Cybernetic Architectures

For the past 50 years, the advancements of technology have equipped architects with unique tools that have enabled the development of new computer-mediated design methods, fabrication techniques, and architectural expressions. Simultaneously, in contemporary architecture new frameworks emerged that have radically redefined the traditional conceptions of design, of the built environment, and of the role of architects.

Cybernetic Architectures argues that such frameworks have been constructed in direct reference to cybernetic thinking, a thought model that emerged concurrently with the origins of informatics and that embodies the main assumptions, values, and ideals underlying the development of computer science. The book explains how the evolution of the computational perspective in architecture has been parallel to the construction of design issues in reference to the central ideas fostered by the cybernetic model. It unpacks and explains this crucial relationship, in the work of digital architects, between the use of information technology in design and the conception of architectural problems around an informational ontology.

This book will appeal to architecture students and scholars interested in understanding the recent transformations in the architectural landscape related to the advent of computer-based design paradigms.

Camilo Andrés Cifuentes Quin is an Architect experienced in architectural design. He is Associate Professor in the Faculty of Habitat Sciences at La Salle University, Bogotá. His research focuses on the impact of information technology in the recent transformations of the architectural landscape and the exploration of computer-based design paradigms in design practice. He holds a Bachelor of Architecture from Los Andes University, Bogotá, a Postgraduate Diploma in Computational Design from ELISAVA (Barcelona School of Design and Engineering), a Masters of Architecture from ENSAG (École Nationale Supériere d'Architecture de Grenoble), and a Ph.D. in Architecture from UPC-Barcelona Tech.

Routledge Research in Architecture

The *Routledge Research in Architecture* series provides the reader with the latest scholarship in the field of architecture. The series publishes research from across the globe and covers areas as diverse as architectural history and theory, technology, digital architecture, structures, materials, details, design, monographs of architects, interior design and much more. By making these studies available to the worldwide academic community, the series aims to promote quality architectural research.

Architectural Anthropology
Exploring Lived Space
Edited by Marie Stender, Claus Bech-Danielsen and Aina Landsverk Hagen

Writing the Materialities of the Past
Cities and the Architectural Topography of Historical Imagination
Sam Griffiths

Louis I. Kahn in Rome and Venice
Tangible Forms
Elisabetta Barizza

Cybernetic Architectures
Informational Thinking and Digital Design
Camilo Andrés Cifuentes Quin

Jørn Utzon and Transcultural Essentialism
Adrian Carter and Marja Sarvimäki

Husserl and Spatiality
Toward a Phenomenological Ethnography of Space
Tao DuFour

For more information about this series, please visit: https://www.routledge.com/Routledge-Research-in-Architecture/book-series/RRARCH

Cybernetic Architectures

Informational Thinking and Digital Design

Camilo Andrés Cifuentes Quin

Routledge
Taylor & Francis Group
LONDON AND NEW YORK

First published 2022
by Routledge
2 Park Square, Milton Park, Abingdon, Oxon OX14 4RN

and by Routledge
605 Third Avenue, New York, NY 10158

Routledge is an imprint of the Taylor & Francis Group, an informa business

British Library Cataloguing-in-Publication Data
A catalogue record for this book is available from the British Library

Library of Congress Cataloging-in-Publication Data
Names: Cifuentes Quin, Camilo Andrés, author.
Title: Cybernetic architectures : informational thinking and digital design / Camilo Andrés Cifuentes Quin, https://orcid.org/0000-0003-1470-9208.
Description: Abingdon, Oxon ; New York : Routledge, 2022. | Series: Routledge research in architecture | Includes bibliographical references and index.
Identifiers: LCCN 2021006291 (print) | LCCN 2021006292 (ebook) | ISBN 9781032019406 (hardback) | ISBN 9781032019420 (paperback) | ISBN 9781003181101 (ebook)
Subjects: LCSH: Architectural design. | Cybernetics.
Classification: LCC NA2750 .C54 2022 (print) | LCC NA2750 (ebook) | DDC 729—dc23
LC record available at https://lccn.loc.gov/2021006291
LC ebook record available at https://lccn.loc.gov/2021006292

ISBN: 978-1-032-01940-6 (hbk)
ISBN: 978-1-032-01942-0 (pbk)
ISBN: 978-1-003-18110-1 (ebk)

DOI: 10.4324/9781003181101

Typeset in Sabon
by KnowledgeWorks Global Ltd.

Contents

Figure 0.1

Preface

Abraham Bosse's illustration "Les perspecteurs," represents three graceful gentlemen who observe three squares that rest on the ground, one square in front of each one of the three men, whose vertexes are attached to four cords that converge in the eye of every observer. Whenever I look at this image, which illustrates the basic principles of monocular linear perspective, what I see, beyond the explanation of the basic rules of perspective, is an expression of the relationship between perspective representation and a vision of the world embodied by the emergence of the liberal subject in western culture. My reading of Bosse's illustration (visibly influenced by the analysis presented by Erwin Panofsky's in his legendary book *Perspective as Symbolic Form*) is representative of a question that underlies the origin of this book and that has accompanied me ever since my early formation years as an architect. As an architecture student, I always wondered what is the link between our worldviews, the objects we design, and the design techniques that we use. The above question became more urgent when, as a junior architect, at the same time that I started using different CAD and 3D modeling tools, I got growingly interested in the work of architects such as Greg Lynn and Peter Eisenman, whose computer-based designs challenged the traditional representations and conceptions of space that I had studied at the school of architecture; in my school, during the late 1990s, the modern paradigm was still considered a model for architectural practice and the post-modern derives were regarded with certain suspicion. Fascinated, as I was, by the radically new visions of architecture and design fostered by the early 1990s digital architects, I got increasingly interested in understanding what conceptions of the world, of the human subject and of the disciplinary problems lay beneath the blobby, monstrous, seamless, and organic-like buildings that by the end of the twentieth century century started to populate the architectural landscape – as new digital design and modeling tools such as Microstation, 3D Studio, Maya, ArchiCad, and FormZ became part of the repertoire of instruments used in architectural design.

With these questions in mind, a few years later, as a graduate student at the *Grenoble School of Architecture*, I undertook the writing of a master's thesis in which I intended to understand the imagination of design fostered by computer mediated architectural practices. Following authors such as Jean François Lyotard and Manuel Castells, with this research I aimed to contribute to the comprehension of the impact of the introduction of information technology in contemporary architectural practice. Through the development of this study, I got to know the ideas of Norbert Wiener as well as the work of various scholars (including Céline Lafontaine, Philippe Breton, Geof Bowker, Armand Mattelart, Peter Gallison, Andrew Pickering, among others) who have studied both the profound influence of cybernetic thinking in contemporary knowledge and the connections between this framework and the origins of computer science. This is how I became aware of the reiterative (and in many cases veiled) references in the work of digital architects to the core ideas exposed in the canonic cybernetic texts. This is also the reason why I decided to look deeper into the connections among cybernetic thinking and the development of the computational perspective in architecture.

My discovery of the frequent references to cybernetic notions in the narratives of computer mediated architectural practices forced me to look for different lenses to analyze the role of digital technology in architectural productions. Since my inquiries led me to study the influence of information discourses as a key aspect of the development of computer-based architectural expressions, it seemed logic that such survey had to overcome the common simplifications of the analyses of the role of technology in cultural productions; namely, the discourses of technological determinism and the visions about the neutrality of technology. While deterministic discourses foster visions of technology as an autonomous and technocratic subject that creates the conditions for cultural change, the visions of technology as a neutral factor see the tools that we use as objects empty of contents waiting for any given use. Both of these two approaches seemed to me insufficient to comprehend the productions of digital architecture, a field which, as I started to notice, redefined the traditional conceptions of space and design on the basis of the introduction in design practice of both the pragmatics and the ontology of the computer. As a matter of fact, a look at the development of the computational perspective in the profession shows that the informatization of architecture has involved a close relation between the technological mediation of design and the creation of new theoretical frameworks informed by a body of knowledge closely related to information discourses. In consequence, I understood that the explorations about the use of information technology in architecture should not be studied only in terms of the mode of praxis that such technology makes possible, but in terms of the way architects have interpreted and translated into architectural knowledge the epistemological and ontological changes underlying the development of computer science.

The above considerations opened a line of inquiry that lead me to the writing of a doctoral dissertation in which I discuss how the dominant visions of computer-based architecture have been grounded not only in the pragmatics of the computer, but in reference to a body of knowledge that makes part of a line of thought that can be traced back to cybernetic theory and the beginnings of informatics. The abovementioned analysis is based on a conceptual framework that permitted me to think of the productions in of digital architecture as expressions that involve a dialogue among technological (information technology) and ideological (information discourses) aspects. Such framework is provided by the modes of analysis of cultural productions developed by scholars such as Bruno Latour, Donna Haraway, and Katherine Hayles, which challenge the comprehension of the technological and the ideological as separate poles. On the contrary, from the perspective of Latour, Haraway, and Hayles, the world of ideas and the world of technique seem to evolve together as a sort of feedback system in which technical advances foster the advent of new conceptual frameworks and vice versa.

Cybernetic Architectures is the result and continuation of the aforementioned research. The book traces the link between the cybernetic paradigm and the conception of buildings as performative, responsive, intelligent, and sentient artifacts; that is, the dominant visions of architectural objects that have shaped the imagination of digital architecture since its beginnings until today. This exploration constitutes a journey through some of the most influential ideas and design models of the recent history of architecture. It is a journey that begins in the 1960s, when a few architects, designers, and technologists in British and American universities started to imagine new design paradigms grounded both in the use of emerging computational technology and informational explanations of architectural issues. Through the different chapters of the book, I will show that, from these early investigations until the most recent expressions of digital architecture, the development of this field can be seen as the evolution of the informational construction of architectural problems.

Through this excursion the reader will discover how the technical and theoretical elaborations of digital architecture have been constructed around a series of ideas inherited from the seminal works of the fathers of cybernetics and from other fields of knowledge – such as operations research, systems thinking, molecular biology, bioinformatics, and complexity theory – that keep a direct relation with the informational paradigm. This account is accompanied by a selection of images which stand out as instances of the imagination of architectural space and design constructed by digital architects. These images are not referenced in the text, but the information about them appears in the table of figures printed at the end of the book. Following a narrative strategy employed by the authors of *Ways of Seeing*, my idea is that the illustrations evoke the themes and ideas expounded in the book, but it is up to the reader to establish the connections.

The final form of this book owes much to Iñaki Abalos' *The Good Life*, an architectural journey in which the author visits the distinctive inventions of the modern house and their relation to the paradigmatic models of thought that emerged along the twentieth century. *The Good Life* is an inspiring work that encouraged me to undertake the writing of these pages. In Abalos' words, it is a contribution to create a better consciousness of the links between the forms of thinking, of seeing the world, the modes of life, and the projective techniques. In the same way, *Cybernetic Architectures* talks about how computer-based design, architecture and by extension, the way humans should live, have been imagined in reference to the key ideas fostered by one of the most influential thought paradigms of the 20th century.

My intellectual debt is also due to various scholars, among them Antoine Picon, Neal Leach, Branco Kolarevic, Christopher Hight, Rivka Oxman, Sean Keller, Altino Joao Rocha, William Mitchell, and Malcolm McCullough, whose investigations about the meeting of digital technology and architectural design have opened different research hints. As a continuation of their efforts, this book is an attempt to trace the intellectual foundations of the ongoing development of a computational perspective in architecture; a necessary approach to promote a critical regard of a field that in recent years has consolidated as a kind of new avant-garde of the profession.

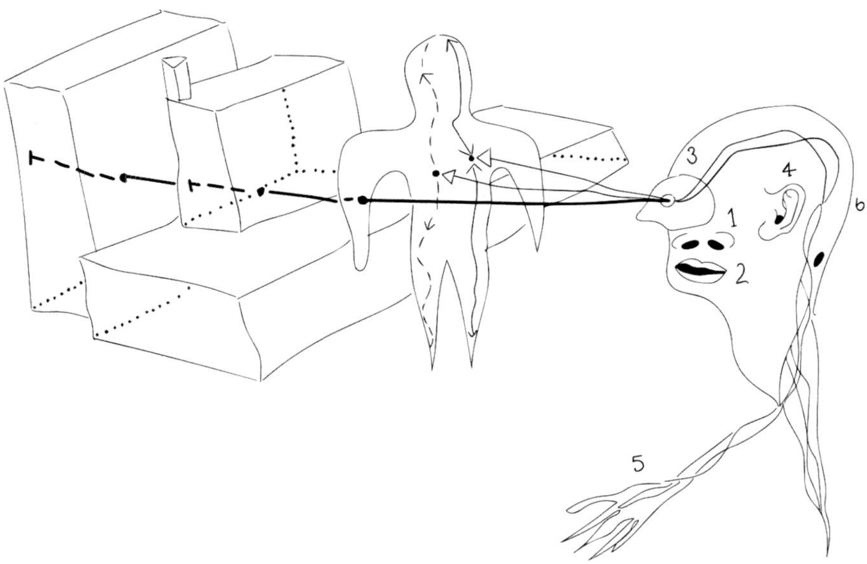

Figure 0.2

Acknowledgments

The completion of *Cybernetic Architectures* was possible thanks to the support of several people and institutions to whom I owe my gratitude. The doctoral research on which the book is based was funded by the *Francisco José de Caldas Grant,* awarded by Colciencias, the extinct Colombian Administrative Department of Science, Technology and Innovation. I am deeply grateful to Colciencias for allowing me the privilege of spending four years of my life devoted exclusively to the sweet labour of learning. The attainment of this scholarship was also possible due to the crucial support of Maria Cecilia O'Byrne, Sandra Corredor, and the staff of the School of Architecture and Design at Los Andes University, who backed my application for the *Francisco José de Caldas Grant*. I am deeply grateful for their help, which was decisive for the start of this journey.

At the Barcelona School of Architecture, which was my academic home during my doctoral studies, I owe a special debt of gratitude to my thesis advisor, Joaquin Regot Marimon, for his constant support and counselling, and to María Ruiz, the secretary of the Graphic Expression Department, who helped me with uncountable demarches that allowed me to focus in my academic work without having to worry much about understanding the bureaucratic aspects of doctoral life at UPC. I am also very grateful to my thesis co-advisor, Pau de Sola Morales, who, since we met at ELISAVA, kindly dedicated many hours of his time to discuss the advances of my research. Many of the ideas exposed in this book are the product of our conversations at the Velodromo Bar.

This work has also benefited from the observations of various readers, some of them anonymous, who commented earlier versions of the arguments presented here; I thank them for their valuable feedback. They include Daniel Cardoso Llach and Rodrigo García Alvarado, who evaluated my doctoral dissertation, as well as the editors and reviewers of the *International Journal of Architectural Computing*, *Leonardo* and *Dearq*, where I have previously published some of the ideas discussed in this book. I thank SAGE Publishing for allowing me to republish some excerpts of the paper "The Cybernetic Imagination of Computational Architecture" published in the *International Journal of Architectural Computing* 14 (2016):

16–29 (appearing partly in revised form in Chapter 1). I thank as well MIT Press for giving me the permission to republish the paper *The Platonic Backhand and Forehand of Cybernetic Architecture* from: Leonardo 52 (2019): 429–434 (appearing partly in revised form in Chapter 6). My gratitude is also due to the organizers of the conferences Materiality in its Contemporary Forms, the International Conference Arquitectonics: Mind, Land, Society, the International Conference on Biodigital Architecture and Genetics, and the IAAC Global Summer School – Quito Lecture Series, coordinated by my friend Seiichi Suzuki, where I have found spaces and pairs to discuss my work.

During my doctoral studies, I had the chance of being invited by Phillippe Liveneau to make part of the teaching team of the master "Ambiances, Architecture, and Culture Numérique" at the Grenoble School of Architecture, in France. I thank him, and the students of the master, for an experience that was enriching both personally and for my research. During those nomad times, in which I lived partly in Barcelona and partly in Grenoble, I was the guest of many dear friends to whom I thank for their hospitality and friendship. Carolina Almeida, Tomás Piquero, David Abondano, Manuela Ianini, Daniel Sadaba, Alvaro Liendo, Ximena Colipan, Gislaine Etié, Dries Verheyen, Sara Bynens, Angélique Gudefin, and Thomas Thivent offered me quite often bed and breakfast. They also comforted me during the difficult times. I thank all the other friends in Barcelona, Grenoble, and Bogotá for making my days outside the libraries.

Across the ocean, at La Salle University, my present academic home, I thank the Faculty of Habitat Sciences for granting me the time required to finish this book. I also thank my colleagues of the LAB LAHC, with whom I have found a stimulating space to think about the digital production of architecture and to make architecture. To my other colleagues and friends from the Faculty of Habitat Sciences, I thank for the refreshing and entertaining talks in the coffee room. Last but not least, I am very grateful to my talented former student, Luisa Gongora, for the beautiful graphic work that accompanies this book. All the images included here were recreated by her.

At Routledge, I thank Francesca Ford, who enthusiastically backed my proposal and invited me to publish this book in the Routledge Research in Architecture series, and Trudy Varcianna, for her help through all the procedural aspects of the publishing process. I also thank the anonymous readers who commented the book proposal and gave me a valuable and positive feedback that helped me to move on with this project.

Finally, my greatest debt is to my family in Colombia and France. To my parents, who taught me the love of books, to my brothers, who have always been there for me, and to my family-in-law, who generously welcomed me as one of them. Céline has been my home during a journey in which we have passed through various cities and too many houses. I dedicate this book to her, who, like some cybernetic architects, is truly committed to making of this world a more coherent and more whole place.

1 Introduction

> Today the World is message, codes and information. Tomorrow what analysis will break down our objects or reconstitute them in a new space? What new Russian doll will emerge?
>
> (François Jacob)

For the past 50 years, the advancements of technology have equipped architects with unique tools that have enabled the development of computer-mediated design methods, digital fabrication techniques, and new architectural expressions that challenge the traditional notions of space and design. Such developments define a well-defined line of research in architecture that I call digital architecture (alternatively called digital design, computer-based architecture, computational design, or computational architecture in the professional and academic circles). The origins of this field can be traced back to the decade of 1960s in some British and American universities, but it has gained momentum during the last four decades – initially thanks to the appearance of the first computer aided design (CAD) software packages and the democratization of computers, and lately due to the growing interest of architects in the exploration of new design and construction methods based on programming, digital fabrication techniques, and other emergent technologies.

In general terms, I use the concept of digital architecture to refer to the architectural practices that have promoted a research agenda engaged with the exploration of the intersection of informatics and design issues. Such practices involve the development of alternative design and construction paradigms based on data analysis as an input of the design process, the use of dynamic procedures to deduce the architectural form in virtual or real environments, the automation of design through the implementation of algorithmic techniques, and the production of space by means of the use of computerized numerical controlled machines. As pointed out by the architectural theorist Branko Kolarevic, globally these investigations include the use of topologic and non-euclidean geometries, the definition of new design methods grounded in genetic, kinetic, and non-linear systems,

DOI: 10.4324/9781003181101-1

and, crucially, the exploration of a connectivity logic in design.[1] In other words, what Kolarevic claims is that the field of digital architecture involves the construction of design issues in reference to new aesthetic and technological considerations, but also in reference to ideological questions. As a matter of fact, since 1960s the investigations of digital architecture have promoted new frameworks and explanations of the disciplinary problems that, in reference to the discourses of information in vogue since the dawn of computer science, have redefined radically the customary conceptions of design, of the built environment, and of the role of architects.

Cybernetic Architectures aims to be a contribution to the comprehension of the shifts of architectural practice connected to the introduction in the profession of information technology during the last decades. With this purpose, the book presents a panorama of the dominant models that have shaped the field of digital architecture since the early investigations on the use of computers, in design until today. The book follows a hint opened by Antoine Picon, who claims that these shifts must be studied from a broader perspective that includes, among other aspects, the attempts to rethink architecture within the cybernetic framework.[2]

Such reading of the field of digital architecture aims to show how some of the most influential visions of design issues fostered by digital architects embody the core ideas of a model of thought that conceives the world as a great system of information exchange. From this perspective, paraphrasing the French biologist François Jacob, it can be claimed that the world of digital architecture is a world of messages, codes, and information. Accordingly, the main interest of this book is to explore to what extent the informational paradigm is the framework within which the computational perspective in architecture has developed. The study focuses on tracing the connections that can be established between the use of information technology in design and the constructions of the disciplinary problems that digital architects have promoted, as they can be deduced from their discourses and projects. As it was mentioned above, such constructions include several crossed references to the key themes promoted by cybernetics and a body of knowledge directly connected to this framework. As we will see, the field of digital architecture has evolved along with the advances of information technology for design and construction, but it has also progressed along with the evolution of cybernetic ideas and the spread of these ideas to different influential theories, thought models and fields of knowledge. So, to comprehend the evolution of digital architecture it is crucial to understand the key cybernetic ideas as well as the cybernetic ascendancy of a body of knowledge that has deeply influenced the productions of digital architects.

To explain the penetration of cybernetic thinking into architectural thinking, I adopt Geof Bowker's concept of "triangulation effect," which describes the cognitive interaction among cybernetics and different fields of knowledge, as well as the primacy of information discourses in contemporary thinking. The comprehension of the transition of cybernetic ideas to a series of theories and scientific models, which in turn enter architectural knowledge, permits to consider the evolution of digital architecture as the result of the feedback among various factors that include disciplinary issues, technical aspects and a variety of references to techno-scientific discourses directly connected to the cybernetic paradigm.

This mode of analysis of digital architecture also draws from the work of scholars such as Bruno Latour, Donna Haraway, and particularly, N. Katherine Hayles, who have attempted different explanations of the construction of knowledge as the product of a permanent feedback among the world of technique and the world of ideas.[3] According to these authors, technology and ideology are two faces of the same coin, and there is not a radical separation between one and the other. In consequence, they challenge the very idea of technological determinism because they show that technology determines cultural productions as much as cultural productions determine the evolution of technology. As a matter of fact, they even deconstruct the idea that there is a difference between culture and technology because from their perspective technology itself appears as a cultural production.

For instance, the mode of analysis proposed by Latour in his influential essay *Nous n'avons jamais été modernes* aims to dismantle the modern myth that suggests that there is a separation between what the author calls the "pole of nature" and the "pole of subject/society"; that is, the supposed division existing between the natural sciences and culture in modern society. In return, the author proposes a reading of the construction of knowledge according to which science and culture converge and define each other in a process that he defines as a "work of mediation."[4] Similarly, Hayles, proposes an approach for analyzing the evolution of knowledge that considers that the permanent feedback between technologies and perceptions (artifacts and ideas) is an essential aspect of the relationship between ideology and technology. According to Hayles, conceptual fields evolve in parallel to material culture due to the constant feedback between concept and artifact.[5] From this perspective, artifacts express the concepts they reproduce and at the same time, the construction of artifacts give way to the formulation of new concepts. Finally, Haraway sketches a theory that designates the social relations between science and technology and that should include "the systems of myth and meanings that structure our imaginations."[6] According to Haraway, "the boundary is permeable between tool and myth, instrument and concept, historical systems of social relations and historical anatomies of possible bodies, including objects of knowledge. Indeed, myth and tool mutually constitute each other."[7]

According to the previous approaches, the restructuring of the world through the social relations of science and technology does not constitute a technological determinism, but it is a system of structured relationships mediated by technology. Then, it is assumed that technology does not determine, but makes possible certain forms of organization. From this perspective, *Cybernetic Architectures* challenges a common trend, among practitioners and critics of digital architecture, to consider technology as an autonomous and central factor that determines and directs the changes in architectural practice. Take, for instance, the introduction to the ACADIA conference *Disciplines & Disruption* held in 2017 at MIT's School of Architecture and Planning, an important research hub in the field of technologically mediated architecture. The organizers introduced the conference by claiming that "For the past 30 years, distinctive advancements in technologies have delivered unprecedented possibilities to architects and enabled new expressions, performance, materials, fabrication and construction processes," and that "Driven by technological, data and material advances, architecture now witnesses the moment of disruption."[8] A similar discourse about the determinant role of technology in the transformation of the discipline appears in a paper recently published by *Design Studies*, where Rivka Oxman, one of the leading theorists of digital design, argues that "emerging media and technology-related models of design have resulted in the rapid development and change of the concepts, content and procedures of digital thinking."[9] In addition, Oxman claims that the early changes in models of design thinking related to the development of computer-based design techniques "occurred first as media technological developments."[10]

The above discourses suggest that the driving force of digital architecture is the advance of information technology. By extension, from these claims it can be deduced that to comprehend the changes in architectural practice connected to the use of emergent technologies the essential element is to understand its technical aspects. At least, they clearly suggest that when it comes to understanding the changes in architectural practice related to the use of new technologies, the technological aspects come first and content follows.

In my opinion, assertions like those cited above are problematic because they obscure the key role that the ideological aspects of the information revolution have played in the construction of the field of digital architecture. Indeed, those claims remind me of a question raised by the French sociologist Philippe Breton. In his history of informatics, he wonders if the comprehension of the integration of informatics in society can be limited to the understanding of the technical aspects of digital technology.[11] The answer he offers is that to limit the study of informatics to its technical aspects would be to negate the scope of the very idea of digital culture. With respect to the study of computer-based architectural practices, Breton's question could be restated in the following terms: can the productions of digital architects be analyzed merely from the comprehension of the technologies they display? The answer that this book offers to this question is the same as the one proposed by Breton. My take is that to reduce the matter of the integration of information technology into architectural practice to its technical aspects would be to deny the profound influence of digital culture in the design professions. To assess such influence, it is fundamental to overcome the deterministic conceptions of the role of technology in design, which leave aside a fundamental aspect of computer-based architectural practices as important as their technical factors; namely, how have been translated into architectural knowledge the epistemological changes and the set of values and ideals embodied by the emergence of information technology.

Crucially, cybernetic thinking – an interdisciplinary framework which emerged from the premise that several phenomena can be explained as information exchange systems – represents the set of values, assumptions and ideals underlying the development of informatics. It is for this reason that the study of cybernetics should be useful to understand the cultural productions grounded on the use of informatics.[12] The former seems quite evident for the study of the field digital architecture, due to the obvious connections that can be established between the emergence of information discourses and information technology. But, in general terms, the comprehension of the cybernetic framework is useful for any study concerned with the transformations of the architectural landscape during the last decades. The reason is that the expansion of cybernetic thinking has been so vast that it is hard to find a field of western knowledge that has not been influenced by this framework – and, as we will see, the influence of cybernetic thinking can be traced in several architectural expressions that do not situate the use of the computer at its core.

In what concerns the evolution of the computational perspective in architecture, the influence of cybernetics is unavoidable. The reason is that since the first explorations about the use of computers in architecture, design issues have been constructed around a series of ideas that evoke the main concepts, ideals, and values advanced by the cybernetic model. For instance, among the themes shared by most practices of digital architecture are the definition of buildings as systems and as self-regulated artifacts, the conception of design as a data-driven process, and the investigation of design methods that explore concepts of automation and artificial intelligence. Last but not least, most practices of digital architecture are grounded on narratives that evoke notions such as information, feedback, homeostasis, system, emergency, self-organization, and complexity, among others. These concepts, which represent the key ideas advanced by the cybernetic model (and also the conceptual changes that took place throughout the development of this framework), are at the core of the dominant models that have directed the evolution of digital architecture. More importantly, they are reminiscent of the evolution of the technical aspects of the digital productions of architecture.

The study of digital architecture demands the understanding of the origin of these narratives and, especially, how they operate in architectural productions; that is, what is the connection between the informational explanations of design issues fostered by digital architects and the artifacts they create. I aim to explain this connection by situating cybernetic thinking as the framework that has directed the visions of the disciplinary problems advanced by digital architects.

To do so, I invite the reader to an excursion through the dominant ideas that have directed the agenda of digital architecture. It is a history that begins in the 1960s when a few architects, designers, and technologists started to imagine, mainly in British and American universities, new design paradigms grounded both in the use of computational technology and the re-conceptualization of design issues in connection to information discourses. Through this journey, the reader will discover to what extent the technical and theoretical elaborations of digital architecture are informed by the main cybernetic concepts.

So, before we start, I propose a brief look at the context in which the cybernetic framework emerged, at the main ideas promoted by cybernetic thinking, and to the factors that explain the vast expansion of this model – which offer clues about the need to adopt a mode of analysis of the productions of digital architecture as a sort of feedback process that involves both the technological mediation of design and a cybernetic imagination of architecture.

In what follows, I will sketch the central ideas of cybernetic theory, with a particular emphasis on the view articulated by the American scientist Norbert Wiener in some of his most influential writings. There are three reasons why I focus particularly on Wiener's ideas. The first is that Wiener is without any doubt the father of this field. He was the first to articulate a theory of cybernetics drawing from the transactions with other pioneers of cybernetic thinking such as Claude Shannon, Warren McCulloch and John von Neumann. The second reason is that I consider Wiener's view the seed of further conceptual shifts that took place during the second half of the twentieth century, and which are embodied by a series of theories and fields of knowledge that make part of the line of thought inaugurated by the first cybernetitians. The third, and most important reason, is that I think that Wiener's cybernetic thinking is particularly representative of the key ideas and assumptions that computer science still embodies today.[13]

The choice of favoring Wiener's vision does not disavow the fact that cybernetic thinking is not the product of a single voice but rather the result of a long conversation that has involved many actors. Wiener's ideas are representative of a particular moment in the history of cybernetics that has come to be called "first-order cybernetics," the period of consolidation of this model, in which notions such as feedback and homeostasis were at the core of the work of the pioneers of cybernetic thinking. Later developments of cybernetic ideas have displaced the research interests of cybernetitians to other notions, such as self-organization and emergence, which are representative of the period known as "second-order cybernetics." More recently, the developments of cybernetic ideas are exemplified by the emergence of the field of artificial life. Through the analysis of the expansion of cybernetic ideas to different fields, which have played a key role in the construction of architectural issues, these later developments of the cybernetic framework will be addressed along the different chapters of the book.

The brief introduction to cybernetic thinking that I will present next does not intend to sketch a comprehensive account of the field of cybernetics (the reader interested in a full history of cybernetics will find attempts in this respect among some of the works cited below). Rather, I will present the central ideas that gave birth to the cybernetic model. This account will allow me to show how this framework spread to almost all fields of western knowledge, which is the key to understand the complex interplay between the informational vision of things and the conceptions of design underlying the discourses and the artifacts conceived by digital architects.

The informational view

It has been widely documented that the 1940s in the United Sates was a decade of frantic scientific research boosted by the military urgencies of World War II;[14] namely, the ballistic control of missiles, the race for the creation of a nuclear fission atomic bomb, the encryption and decryption of war messages, and the necessity to construct powerful computing machines able to process the vast amounts of data required by these projects.

It was in this context that cybernetic thinking emerged. As a matter of fact, several distinguished researchers that played a central role in the consolidation of both computer science and the cybernetic model were involved in different projects funded by the military apparatus, particularly in the United States and England that made part of the war efforts made by these countries during World War II. Among these researchers were Norbert Wiener, the main promoter of cybernetic thinking, Alan Turing, the famous British mathematician who set the ground for the development of computer science, and John von Neumann, responsible for groundbreaking work in the field of computer science. Wiener was involved in research on fire control, Turing was implicated in different cryptanalysis projects, and von Neumann was responsible for the creation of the first digital computer – besides his key part in the conception of the first computers, von Neumann was a fierce supporter of the Manhattan Project.[15]

In connection with the trendy research subjects of the mid twentieth century, cybernetic thinking was born from the basic premise that several natural and artificial phenomena, from computing machines to the functioning of social groups, can be explained as information processing systems. Not surprisingly, this framework embodies the central assumptions, values, and ideals underlying the development of computer science. The reason why cybernetics and computer science share this common ground is that both fields emerged concurrently, and the main characters involved in the development of one field usually appear in the stories of the development of the other.

In the case of the origins of cybernetics, the consolidation of this model as a well-defined field of research was the outcome of the transactions (that came to be known later as the *Macy Conferences on Cybernetics*[16]) among a group of prominent scientists – coming from diverse fields that included circuit analysis, logic, neuroscience, anthropology, and biology – who shared a common interest; namely, the use of concepts of communication science to the particular problems of their respective disciplinary fields.[17] For this reason, during the 1940s and the 1960s the promoters of the cybernetic model discussed the same problems and themes discussed by the then nascent field of computer science. These discussions involved concepts such as logic, control, regulation, recursion, programing, complexity, and feedback, and their application to research problems in fields as diverse as biology and anthropology. More importantly, the exchanges among the first cybernetitians revolved around an idea that was central to the work of early computer scientists such as Alan Turing and John von Neumann. I refer to the belief, shared by several researchers of the time, that the functioning of information processing machines was equivalent to that of living systems. That is why it is not casual that, just like computer science, the cybernetic view of things has been erected on narratives such as the comparison between the computer and the brain, the conception of computing machines as potential surrogates of humans, and the opinion that logic is an universal value and a tool to understand and transform the world.[18]

Behind these narratives is an idea of deep ontological and epistemological implications that gained momentum after the second half of the twentieth century and still exerts a profound influence in the construction of knowledge in the present time. I refer to the widely spread belief that the essence of several phenomena is information, or more precisely, the exchange of information. In a certain way, the story of the emergence of cybernetics is the story of how information became the central concept of an era.[19]

The informational vision of things consolidated in reference to a series of themes exposed in the work of contemporary prominent scientists such as Claude Shannon's communication theory, Ludwig von Bertalanffy's general systems theory, Warren McCulloch's model of the brain as an information processing system, and John von Neumann's work on binary processors (to name just some of the most influential investigations that shaped the information paradigm). All these ideas converged into a theory of universal pretentions articulated by Norbert Wiener, the most famous and principal promoter of cybernetic thinking.[20]

Wiener used the term "cybernetic" to describe those systems capable of self-regulating their behavior due to their ability to process the information they receive from their environment and whose action, inversely, has an impact on their surroundings. According to this definition, all systems that involve recursive processes of cause and effect that work in circular loops are cybernetic, be them servomechanisms, animals, or humans. This circular logic derives from the notion of "negative feedback." In communication sciences, this concept describes the process by which "the increase in the value of a quantity tends to produce a decrease of that quantity (or the other way around)"[21] that produces "the stable value of the quantity, resistant to environmental perturbations."[22] In more simple words, negative feedback is a mechanism that consists of introducing into a system an action proportional to the output of the system, so that the conditions of the system remain stable. The thermostat is the perfect example to explain negative feedback; it is a mechanism that permits to keep stable the temperature of a given system by means of turning it off and on as its temperature is larger or lower to a given value (as it happens in an oven, a refrigerator or an air conditioning system).

The logic of circular causality described by the notion of negative feedback is perhaps the most important element of cybernetic thinking. Drawing from this idea, Wiener and his colleagues imagined a framework to analyze diverse phenomena as communicational forms of organization, as feedback systems whose actions produce changes on their environment, that subsequently trigger changes on them.[23] Although the concept of negative feedback describes a very specific engineering problem, cyberneticians used it to explain a great variety of scientific problems; particularly Wiener, who situated this engineering notion at the basis of a new conception of the world. For Wiener, the universe as a whole is a sort of negative feedback system.

This conception of things was developed by Wiener in two of his most influential books: *Cybernetics: Or Control and Communication in the Animal and the Machine* and *The Human Use of Human Beings*. In these writings Wiener elaborates on a series of ideas that appeared for the first time in an article titled *Behavior, purpose, and teleology* published in 1943 by *Philosophy of Science*. This seminal article contains the ground of Wiener's cybernetic theory, and it was co-authored by the Mexican physiologist Arturo Rosenblueth and Julian Bigelow, an electrical engineer who worked with Wiener on the application of negative feedback to fire control for anti-aircraft guns during the war (this research, in which Wiener and Bigelow conceptualized the relation among the enemy jet pilots and the gunners as a kind of feedback system, was central to the development of some of the key elements of Wiener's thought).[24]

In *Behavior, purpose, and teleology*, Wiener, Rosenblueth, and Bigelow defined a behaviorist approach to study natural and artificial phenomena and to classify their behavior. More precisely, they defined a study of behavior that was restricted to the analysis of the impact of external events (inputs) and the observed changes (outputs) resulting from such external events in a given system. Here it should be noted that the mode of analysis proposed by the authors translates the basic elements of communication theory into categories that are generalized to the study of problems that exceed the domain of communication science. This move allowed them to conclude that "a uniform behavioristic analysis is applicable to both machines and living organisms, regardless of the complexity of the behavior."[25] More importantly, this black-box approach permitted the authors to elude the obvious differences among natural and artificial systems. This was a groundbreaking development because it set the basis to erase the limits between life sciences and engineering. By means of the demonstration that living systems and machines could be analyzed and classified under the same categories, Wiener and his colleagues started a scientific revolution that would change the world of knowledge, and whose impact can still be perceived in contemporary cultural practices.[26]

In later writings, Wiener took to another level the basic premise exposed in *Behavior, purpose, and teleology;* that is, the proposal of studying from the same perspective natural and artificial systems. For instance, this idea takes on a more radical tone when Wiener claims that humans, natural systems, and servomechanisms are similar forms of organization whose functioning depends on communication mechanisms. This point is central to the argument of *Cybernetics*, where Wiener argues that, from the cybernetic perspective, the problems of communication and control are inherent to the notion of message, be it transmitted by electrical, mechanic, or nervous means.[27] Through this assertion, Wiener aims to a double target. On the one hand, he postulates that the transmission of information is a central aspect of various phenomena of scientific interest, independently of their nature. On the other hand, he presents cybernetic theory as the framework that can provide the conceptual and epistemological apparatus to study, produce, or think about phenomena whose essence is the exchange of information. Accordingly, Wiener describes cybernetic theory as, "the study of messages as a means of controlling machinery and society, the development of computing machines and other such automata, certain reflections upon psychology and the nervous system, and a tentative new theory of scientific method."[28]

Differently to the model presented in *Behavior, purpose, and teleology,* the framework described in *Cybernetics* and *The Human Use of Human Beings* was far more ambitious. It was not limited to the definition of an analysis method of communicational phenomena; it described an entirely new vision of things that, in the end, implied the construction of a new kind of science. This new kind of science needed a conceptual scaffolding that Wiener constructed in reference to two key notions that complement (and explain) the central role of the concept of information in cybernetic thinking. Such notions are entropy and feedback.

Information, feedback, and entropy

For Wiener, the study of the communicational nature of things had a clear-cut objective, namely, to fight entropy. The cybernetitian inherited this idea form the American scientist Josiah Willard Gibbs, who made important contributions to the field of physical chemistry in base of applications of thermodynamics, and who created the field of statistical mechanics along with James Clerk Maxwell and Ludwig Boltzmann. According to Gibbs, in the measure that the universe gets older, it heads for a state of maximum disorder. Wiener explains that the measure of that possibility is entropy, a phenomenon characterized by its tendency to grow indefinitely. Gibbs' description of the universe as an entropic system stems from one of the most important principles of nineteenth century physics, namely, the second law of thermodynamics. This law establishes that the entropy of a closed system never decreases; on the contrary, it evolves naturally towards thermodynamic equilibrium, that is, towards a state of maximum disorder.

Despite the inexorable movement of the universe towards chaos, for Wiener there are territories where organization tends to grow: "while the universe as a whole, if indeed there is a whole universe, tends to run down, there are local enclaves whose direction seems opposed to that of the universe at large and in which there is a limited and temporary tendency for organization to increase. Life finds its home in some of these enclaves."[29] For the cybernetitian, organisms, and by extension all communicational phenomena, including servomechanisms, are systems that display processes of decreasing entropy. From the cybernetic perspective, the key to understand these system's capacity to resist the force of entropy is the fact that they are not closed systems, because they exchange information with a given environment – and that is the reason why in cybernetic thinking, the circulation of information is considered to be the essence of the organization of diverse communicational phenomena. So, if Wiener considered cybernetic thinking as a science of regulation and control of communicational systems, he also considered this framework as a tool to combat the natural tendency of the world towards entropy.

At this point appears the central role of the notion of feedback in Wiener's thought. If entropy is a measure of disorganization, then "the information carried by a set of messages is a measure of organization. In fact, it is possible to interpret the information carried by a message as essentially the negative of its entropy."[30] From the above it follows that the exchange of information has a very precise purpose. For Wiener, this mechanism is the condition of existence of any open system: to receive and to use the information acquired from the context is a requirement for the adaptation of any system to a given environment. This idea is clearly expressed by one of Wiener's most famous maxims: "to live effectively is to live with adequate information."[31]

The previous idea is inseparable from the question of regulation, which is the central issue behind the concept of feedback in cybernetic theory. We have seen before that if the interchange of messages defines a form of organization, then the information contained in a message is the measure of the organization of any given system. This means that in any system capable of exchanging information with the environment and other systems, the information exchanged is the regulatory element that permits the system to keep a state of equilibrium. And, since this regulation process is an internal mechanism, cybernetic phenomena are considered to be self-regulated phenomena. Feedback is therefore the mechanism that allows a system to self-regulate its behavior. To be precise, feedback is the process that allows communicational systems to modify their behavior according to the information they obtain from the outside world (this includes the information regarding the transformations that take place in the outside world due to the system's impact, as in an air conditioning system). In *Behavior, purpose and teleology*, feedback is described exactly in these terms, that is, as the mechanism that allows a system to use the outputs of a given process as inputs of the system. Importantly, according to the method described by Wiener, Rosenblueth, and Bigelow, feedback is a common feature, and the key aspect, of the functioning of both natural systems and communication machines. From this perspective, processes such as regulation, learning, and adaptation depend on the feedback mechanisms that permit organisms and machines to acquire information from the world and to transform it into valid information for the operation of the system.

If the construction of information as the essence of several phenomena defined a new ontology of things that erased the limits between natural systems and machines, the conceptualization of the nature of the exchange among different systems as a feedback mechanism was probably the most important contribution of cybernetics to contemporary epistemology. Since the publication in 1948 of *Cybernetics*, this idea has been on the ground of the conception of several phenomena as systems governed by the logic of circular causality. As explained by Peter Gallison, from the moment Wiener conceived the enemy jet pilots like a sort of feedback machine that could be simulated electronically, it only took a short step "to thinking of the Allied gunner in the same way. Then human psychology began to appear as a cybernetic system, then the human mind, then life, then even the world system as a whole."[32] As a matter of fact, from the second half of the twentieth century, the research in several fields that include computer science as well as the ensemble of natural and social sciences have been informed by cybernetic notions. As a result, in practically all fields of western knowledge, including architecture, emerged informational explanations of natural, social and physical phenomena that evoke a series of cybernetic narratives that we take for granted today.

In what follows, I will sketch a brief explanation of the reasons why (and the means by which) the cybernetic ideas spread to the extent that even the world system as a whole eventually began to be conceived as a cybernetic system. As mentioned before, the expansion of the cybernetic framework is crucial to comprehend the productions of digital architects. For the explanation, I will draw from the hypotheses advanced by Phillippe Breton in this sense, but mainly from the work of Geof Bowker, who has described the cognitive interaction among cybernetics and different fields of knowledge as the product of a "triangulation effect."

The triangulation effect

In a book titled *L'utopie de la communication,* the French sociologist Phillippe Breton traces the impact of information discourses in contemporary culture, and he offers an explanation of the vast spread of cybernetic ideas. For Breton, cybernetic theory is not only a scientific model. It is a utopic vision of society grounded on the idea of communication that has had a tremendous influence in different fields of science and technology, but also in the cultural, political and social spheres.[33]

As we have seen, cybernetic theory fosters the idea that several phenomena can be understood in terms of relations, in terms of the exchange and circulation of information. Breton reminds that together with this idea, Wiener promoted an agenda that exceeded the scope of a scientific project. This agenda included promoting a new anthropological definition of the human being and placing communication as the central value of society. In addition, it was connected to three imperatives: the recognition of humans as communicating beings, assigning a new status to machines in society, and converting society into a self-regulating system thanks to the open character of the communication channels. According to Breton, it was by means of these discourses that Wiener and his colleagues managed to make of communication a concept of great social and political scope, which explains the expansion of cybernetic thinking.

As a matter of fact, the strategy was successful because in a few years the informational view of things became dominant, and it raised as the paradigm that directed the research problems of different disciplines. For Breton, the rise of cybernetics as the model that directed the development of other fields guaranteed the expansion of information discourses in a double sense. On one side, the informational explanation of things provided the concepts that several disciplines used to define their research problems. In this way, a series of biological, physical, and social phenomena started to be conceived as communicational systems. Breton claims that these explanations constitute the second element that explains the expansion of cybernetic thinking. For Breton, the construction of various phenomena of scientific interest as informational systems became was one the most important vehicles for the dissemination of cybernetic narratives, which transited from the world of science to the world of popular culture via popular science books and science fiction. The paradigmatic example of this transference process is the construction of the mechanisms of heredity as a programed system. Although most people may not know nothing about the cybernetic origins of the concept of "genetic code," most of us are used to think of our genes as carriers of information that determine several aspects of our lives (any reader of Richard Dawkins, or any kid who has watched an episode of X-men, is aware of this idea).

The sociologist of science and technology Geoffrey Bowker has come to conclusions similar to those advanced by Breton. In a study of the rhetoric strategies employed by the cyberneticians to legitimize the informational approach, Bowker argues that the promoters of cybernetics managed to make of this model the framework that directed the development of other fields of knowledge. As explained in his article, *How to be Universal: Some Cybernetic Strategies, 1943–70*, Bowker suggests that the expansion of information discourses was possible due to three interconnected traits of cybernetic theory. First of all, cybernetics offered a new reading of human history. Second, it displayed a language that facilitated such reading. Finally, through the generalization of cybernetic language, cybernetic theory provided the means to legitimize a new labor division in scientific practice.[34]

In what concerns the first aspect, Bowker points out that Wiener had the capacity to talk about very specific issues and to use the same ideas to talk about very general questions. He explains, for example, that in *Behavior, Purpose and Teleology* the strategy was to produce a taxonomy of different types of behavior and then to show that animals and machines could be situated on both sides of each division. In this way, when Wiener and his colleagues described organisms and machines as analog systems (based on their shared communicational nature), they could claim both the emergence of a new kind of science and the advent of a new era, that of the "form and the synchronic structure of information."[35]

Under the motto of the arrival of a new era, the cybernetitians addressed a number of themes unrelated to the problems of science. For instance, in *God and Golem inc*, Wiener examines a series of situations "which have been discussed in religious books and have a religious aspect, but possess a close analogy to other situations which belong to science, and in particular to the new science of cybernetics, the science of communication and control, whether in machines or living organisms."[36] Wiener also discussed political issues connected to the dangers of technological advance, including irresponsible automation and the production of nuclear weapons, and he postulated cybernetics as the means to prevent such dangers. For Bowker, this strategy permitted the cybernetitians to claim the arrival of a new era in two ways: conjuncturally, in what concerns the advance of science and technology, and ideologically, by proposing ideas of great social and political scope.

Here appears the second aspect mentioned by Bowker. The rise of a new paradigm of thought had to be stated somehow, and the cybernetic notions (message, information, self-regulation, feedback, entropy) accomplished this function. More importantly, these concepts constituted the means that guaranteed the exchange among different fields of knowledge. Bowker claims that a researcher which fostered an extravagant argument gained legitimacy when he made reference to other investigations that displayed similar arguments: "an isolated scientific worker making an outlandish claim could gain rhetorical legitimacy by pointing to support from another field - which in turn referenced the first worker's field to support its claims."[37] This mechanism of transference is what Bowker calls "triangulation effect."

Via the triangulation effect, the cybernetic language offered new forms of cognitive interaction among diverse investigations. In this manner, the ideas and tools developed in one field could be employed to explain problems of a different nature in another discipline (biological ideas could be introduced in physics and vice-versa) and the language of cybernetics "made the work of smoothing the discontinuity."[38] A classic example of the former is computer scientists' description of the computer as a sort of artificial brain. Computer scientists could claim that computation and the neural system worked in similar ways thanks to the investigations of neuroscientists that, inversely, had explored the idea that the brain could be described as a sort of information processing system. The argument of computer scientists does not only gain legitimacy thanks to the neuroscientists' research, but it also helps to make more credible the proposal of considering the brain as a computer.

According to Bowker, it was this mechanism of transference of concepts what permitted the expansion of cybernetic thinking, and it was by this means that the cybernetic objective of reorganizing the scientific practice was achieved. As he concludes, these strategies permitted cybernetics to "operate either as the primary discipline, directing others on their search for truth, or as a discipline providing analytic tools indispensable to the development and progress of others. At both the superstructural and infrastructural level, the rhetoric held that cybernetics was unavoidable if one wanted to do meaningful, efficient science."[39]

Interestingly, the mechanism of cognitive interaction that explains the spread of cybernetics is at the hearth of the productions of digital architecture. As we will see, the explorations of digital architects are informed by a series of techniques, theories, and notions directly inherited from cybernetic theory or from a variety of fields in which cybernetics has been either the primary discipline or the discipline that has provided the tools for their development. For this reason, the concept of triangulation effect is quite useful to think about the evolution of digital architecture. This notion is helpful to understand the cybernetic background of the dominant narratives of digital architecture, but also to comprehend how these narratives have allowed the development of new design methods that, inversely, have fostered new informational constructions of design issues.

The triangulation effect in digital architecture

The process that Bowker calls "triangulation effect" has been fundamental to the development of digital architecture. In this field, the influence of cybernetics can be clearly observed in several constructions of architectural issues that, since the mid twentieth century, have been grounded on explanations of architecture as a sort of communicational phenomenon.

Through the description of the built environment as a reality that emerges from the constant interaction among diverse elements, architects have conceptualized buildings as systems governed by the logic of circular causality. This narrative has permitted them to establish analogies between architectural matters and the research problems of different fields of knowledge informed by cybernetics. Inversely, through this move, the concepts and techniques employed in these fields to study a variety of phenomena have been integrated into architectural knowledge. Back in the 1960's this cognitive interaction operated as follows. By comparing the built environment to a feedback system, architects started to employ cybernetic notions to think of the problems of architecture; a move that led some of them to use emerging computational techniques to solve design problems.[40] Ever since, this kind of dynamic has been at the core of the development of the technical means (informed by computer science) and the conceptual frameworks (informed by cybernetic notions) that have shaped the evolution of digital architecture.

Given the context of the development of cybernetics and computer science, it comes as no surprise that, with the introduction of information technology in architectural practice, the productions of computer-mediated design evoke the research problems, values and ideals shared by computer science and the cybernetic framework. As mentioned above, both fields emerged concurrently, and various scholars have explained how these two fields appeared in response to the socio-political conditions of the Second World War and Postwar America.

In this context, both cybernetics and computer science were grounded on a set of shared aspects, which included the ambition of computer scientists to produce intelligent and autonomous systems, as well as the cyberneticians proposal to consider from the same perspective servomechanisms and natural systems. Since the early explorations of digital architecture, these shared ideals have been embodied by the work of digital architects – who have fostered both the use of computational techniques and the construction of new architectural frameworks grounded on information discourses. This basic observation highlights the relevance of two interrelated points central to the argument of this book.

The first point is that the study of the role that the introduction of information technology has played in the transformations of architectural practice cannot be restricted to the analysis of the technical aspects of computer-based productions. On the contrary, since computing is considered here as a technical event that embodies an informational ontology and epistemology, the study of its introduction in architecture has to take into account the set of values and ideals that this technology embodies. At this point appears the second central element of my argument. In the same way that information technology cannot be understood independently from the set of values it embodies, the productions of digital architecture cannot be explained simply from the analysis of the introduction of computer pragmatics in design. The informational construction of design issues has been as important as the introduction of information technology for the consolidation of the research agenda of digital architecture. Therefore, any account of its productions and of its consolidation has to explain the cognitive interactions among architecture, information discourses and information technology that have shaped this field.

Interestingly, the migration of information discourses into architectural thinking was not necessarily the outcome of the exploration of the use of computer pragmatics in design. As a matter of fact, the influence of cybernetic ideas was crucial for the development of some of the most influential (pre-digital) architectural explorations of the late twentieth century. Among them can be mentioned Cedric Price's projects for interactive buildings, the mega-structural movement's proposal to blur the distinction between architecture and the city, as well as the metabolist's organic conception of architecture and of urban space. In this respect, Antoine Picon argues that the cybernetic paradigm was also connected to some of the leading explorations of late modernism, which include the emergence of design methods grounded on typological research as well as those explorations based on the manipulation of geometrical patterns and systems of signs.[41]

Although the above-mentioned explorations did not always situate the use of information technology at the core of architectural research, many of them can be connected to some early paradigmatic investigations on the use of informatics in architecture. Think, for instance, of the collaboration among Price and the British Cybernetitian Gordon Pask, the relation between the work of Yonna Friedman and the investigations of Nicholas Negroponte's *Architecture Machine Group*, or the connections that can be established between the explorations of late modernism and the work of influential digital architects and digital design theorists, such as Peter Eisenman and William Mitchell.

The connections that can be established between pre-digital and digital architectural expressions that foster an informational view of the disciplinary problems reinforce the idea that the cybernetic model is a key element to understand the emergence and evolution of digital architecture. This

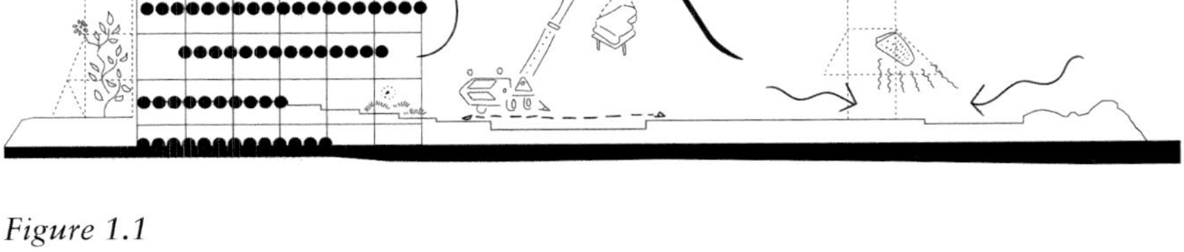

Figure 1.1

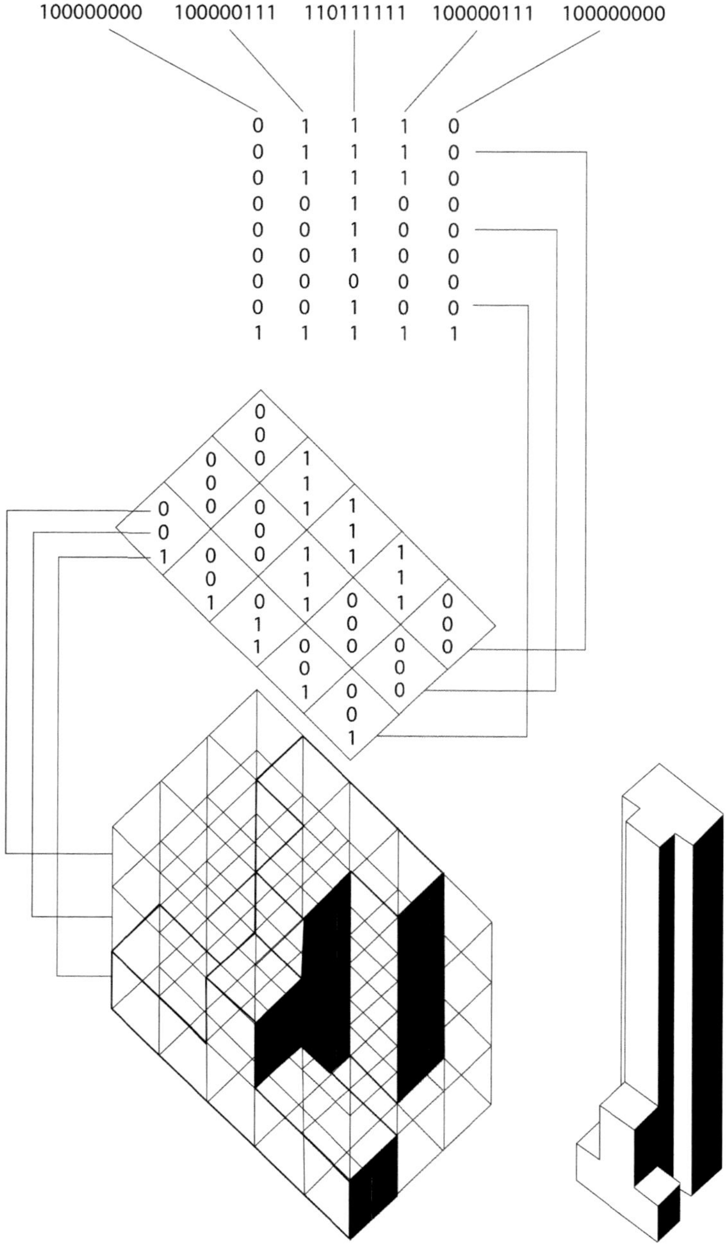

Figure 1.2

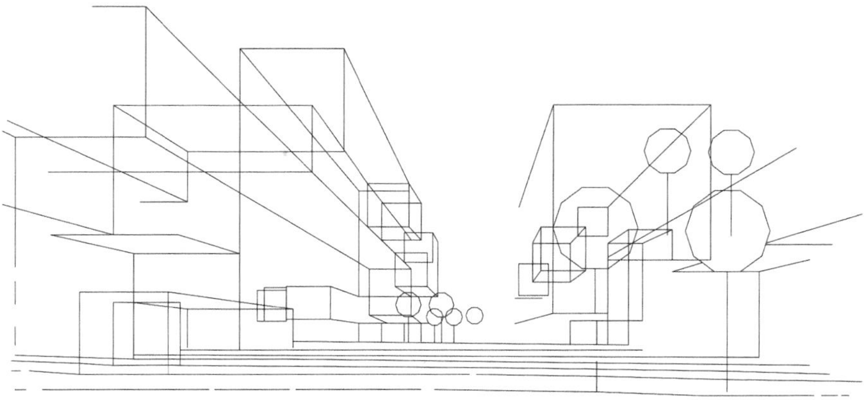

Figure 1.3

idea becomes quite more evident if one takes into account that the seminal investigations of computer-based design endorsed a cybernetic imagination of design issues; some paradigmatic examples are Ivan Sutherland's *Sketchpad*, the investigations developed at *LUBFS*, as well as the above-mentioned research agenda of Negroponte's *Architecture Machine Group*.

In this respect, different scholars have pointed out how the early explorations of digital architecture were informed by cybernetic principles or by scientific notions inherited from connected fields such as structuralism, operations research, linguistics, and systems analysis.[42] This is the reason why some of the first expressions of digital architecture embody conceptions of architectural objects and design as communicational phenomena, as self-regulating systems that display mechanisms of circular causality. From then until now, the productions in the field of digital architecture have been often based on informational constructions of design problems that evoke notions inherited from a series of scientific models and theories that include systems theory, molecular biology, bioinformatics, and complexity science, among other fields connected to the cybernetic paradigm. The corollary of these constructions of architectural issues has been the development of computer-based design methods in which the production of space is considered a problem-solving question, an emergent reality resulting from the dynamic interactions among several elements, or an algorithmic procedure that mimics the formation processes of natural systems.

Taking the above into account, it is possible to assert that to talk about the development of the computational perspective in architecture is to talk about the migration of cybernetic ideas into the body of knowledge of the profession. From the perspective of New Media studies, the former observation seems rather obvious, since for New Media theorists, the "computerization" of cultural productions implies a "transcodification" of cultural categories. In this respect, Lev Manovich argues that in computer-mediated cultural productions the traditional categories are replaced by other categories that stem not only from the pragmatics of the computer, but from the ontology and epistemology inherent to the development of computer science.[43] From the above it follows that the analysis of computer-mediated cultural productions implies to study them both as technical and ideological events.

Some architectural critics and theorists have adopted a similar mode of analysis. Accordingly, they acknowledge that the study of the evolution of the computational perspective in architecture must consider the concurrent development of new techniques and new theoretical frameworks. Even Oxman, who has advanced deterministic explanations of digital architecture has claimed that, "perhaps the most challenging of the conditions created by the emergence of new technologies of digital design ... has been the simultaneous emergence of new theoretical and philosophical frameworks that constitute the intellectual foundations of digital design."[44] The aim of this book is to reveal to what extent such frameworks stem from the cybernetic model. To do so, the productions of digital architecture will be considered here as a "seriation," in reference to the mode of analysis proposed by Hayles to study the evolution of cybernetics, which considers the parallel evolution of the world of technique and the world of ideas as a sort of feedback system.

Digital architecture as a seriation

As mentioned before, Hayles uses the term "seriation," borrowed from archaeological anthropology, to describe the parallel evolution of the technical aspects and conceptual fields in the development of cybernetic thinking. Hayles explains that "Conceptual fields evolve similarly to material culture, in part because concept and artifact engage each other in continuous feedback loops. An artifact materially expresses the concept it embodies, but the process of its construction is far from passive. A glitch has to be fixed, a material exhibits unexpected properties, an emergent behaviour surfaces – any of these challenges can give rise to a new concept, which results in another generation of artifact, which leads to the development of still other concepts."[45] This mode of analysis – that recalls the explanations of technological development promoted by Latour and Haraway – considers the production of knowledge as a kind of feedback system. From this perspective, the evolution of knowledge is the product of a system of circular causality, in which the conceptual fields evolve hand in hand with the material culture.

The notion of seriation is ideal to explain the evolution of a field like digital architecture, whose expressions, as we have seen, must be considered both as technical and ideological events. The evolution of digital architecture matches perfectly the idea that concepts and artifacts engage each other in continuous feedback loops. According to this mode of analysis, I will explore further the connection between the investigations about the use of computers in architecture and the construction of cybernetic explanations of architectural problems. Through this survey, I will show that at the same time that architects started to explore uses of information technology in design, they started to imagine architecture as a sort of informational phenomenon – introducing into architectural explanations concepts imported from cybernetics and other connected fields of knowledge. In this way, I will show that this change of paradigm in the explanations of architecture fostered the exploration of new computer-based design methods, while new constructions of architecture were developed in direct reference to cybernetic ideas. *Cybernetic Architectures* presents the emergence and evolution of the dominant models of digital architecture as the outcome of this circular logic. From this perspective, the book shows how the cybernetic imagination of architecture has fostered the elaboration of computer-based design tools and methods, while the technological mediation of architecture has boosted the construction of informational explanations of disciplinary issues, which in turn have triggered the search of new computational design paradigms, and so on.

The journey through the architectural ideas and projects that will be visited in the following chapters, aims to analyze how this feedback process works; namely, how the core ideas of cybernetic thinking migrated to the various fields of knowledge that have informed the dominant models of digital architecture, how the notions inherited from these fields have been integrated into architectural knowledge, and how the resulting visions of architectural issues have conditioned, and have been conditioned by, the use and development of information technology for architectural design.

Chapter outline

In Chapter 2, I discuss the centrality of the concept of performance in early investigations of computer-based design approaches. The analysis shows the connection between this notion and the emergence of cybernetic conceptions of buildings (as responsive, self-regulated, communicational artifacts, and of architectural design as an information-driven practice) still in force today. In order to illustrate the influence of cybernetic thinking in the first explorations of applications of informatics in architectural practice, I trace the cybernetic ascendancy of the performative conception of architecture, an ontology of the disciplinary problems that has been at the core of the investigations of digital design since the origins of this line of research. To do so I visit different definitions of the concept of performance in architecture, and I discuss the role of the cybernetic framework in *Performance Design*, a seminal computer-based design model presented in 1967 by the journal *Progressive Architecture*.

Drawing from this survey, in the second part of Chapter 2, I explain how, by embracing the discourses of performance, several contemporary expressions of digital architecture have endorsed the cybernetic imagination of design issues promoted by the pioneers of this field. Thereby, I also explain the relationship between the performative view and the technological base of computational design, as well as its connection with new conceptions of architectural space and of the inhabitant inherent to the work of digital architects, which embody the informational conception of things. Through this analysis, I show that the paradigmatic expressions of digital architecture return recursively to the same themes (the conception of buildings as dynamic systems, as devices highly integrated with the environment, as communicational and sentient artifacts ruled by flows of information).

According to this observation, I claim that the concept of performance is a key element to comprehend the evolution of digital design thinking. From this starting point, in the next chapters, I attempt to show how the performative/cybernetic view is at the core of the dominant models of digital architecture. I classify these models according to three categories (architectural systems, genetic mechanisms, and complex phenomena) that are described in relation to their connection to different scientific theories, concepts, or disciplines that inform them (systems thinking, molecular biology and bioinformatics, and complexity theory respectively). My account of these models is based on the same narrative strategy. After situating the connection between the problems of architecture and a given model or discipline of reference, I present a brief description of the main ideas promoted by the corresponding model of reference and of its connection to the cybernetic framework. Further, I explain how architectural issues have been constructed in reference to the ideas, concepts and techniques inherited from the reference models.

In Chapter 3, I analyze the influence on digital architecture of systems thinking, a scientific model that, in line with the informational conception of things fostered by the cybernetitians, endorsed the conception of a variety of physical, biological, and social phenomena as interconnected forms of organization whose essence is in the relations they keep with a given environment. The construction of design issues in reference to this paradigm of thought has been a common theme of digital architecture since the inception of performance-based design models, where architectural design was imagined as a subsidiary practice of fields such as operations research and systems analysis. In the first part of this chapter, drawing from the main writings of Ludwing von Bertalanffy and other systems thinkers such as Ervin Laszlo and Edgar Morin, I expose the central ideas of systems theory, and I explain the connection between these ideas and the cybernetic paradigm.

In the second part of this chapter, I discuss the connection between systems thinking and the construction, in computer-based design practices, of architectural objects as totalities, as integrated phenomena and as autonomous devices. In addition, I discuss the connection between the systems view and the discourses about the autonomy of architecture, quite common in practices of digital design. From this analysis I establish the link between the systems view and a distinctive aspect of several explorations of digital architecture; namely, the construction of design problems in reference to biological metaphors. Following the lead of the cybernetic origins of the "biologization" of architecture in digital design practices, in the following chapters, I analyze the construction of architectural objects as programmed systems and as self-organized emergent phenomena.

In Chapter 4, I explore the centrality of informational thinking in contemporary biology and the significance of this paradigm shift in natural sciences for the consolidation of morphogenetic design models in architecture. To situate this connection, In the first part of this chapter, I explain the relationship among cybernetics and the rise of informational representations of nature, as represented by the stories about the origins of the construction of heredity as an information code – which make part of the cultural production of post-war America. Drawing from this survey, in the second part of this chapter, I trace the transit of the informational descriptions of organisms to architectural expressions grounded on genetic design models. I explain how these models are grounded, on the one hand, on the development of digital design methods inspired on the techniques of computational biology, and, on the other hand, on the construction of analogies between the algorithmic production of architecture and the contemporary explanations of biological phenomena such as genetic coding, evolution, development, and adaptation.

In this way, I show the cybernetic ascendancy of the architectural discourses and techniques that have constructed buildings as programmable artifacts and, in some utopian visions, as semi-organic machines ruled by the same principles as living systems that could eventually form and create themselves. Through this survey, I explain how genetic design approaches reenact the performative conception of the built environment and the ambitions of autonomy inherent to the work of many digital architects.

The above is the starting point of Chapter 5, in which I explain how the complexity paradigm has become the framework to think of a radically emergent architecture. In this chapter, I discuss the connection between complexity thinking and recent explorations of digital design that I call emergent design models, which have introduced into architectural explanations (via complexity discourses) the main themes of the second and third waves of cybernetics. Drawing from an account of the central ideas and concepts of complexity science, and of the connections of this framework to cybernetic thinking, I show that the discourses and methods of emergent design models are grounded on the construction of the architectural object as a kind of complex system. In this way, I explain how emergent design models construct architectural objects as self-organized forms of organization which emerge from the exchanges among several interconnected elements without the intervention of an organ of central control. In addition, I show to what extent this vision of architectural issues revisits the recurrent themes that digital architects have exploited since the 1960s.

With this analysis, I complete my picture of the evolution of digital architecture from the perspective of the penetration of informational thinking in the profession; it is a kind of pointillist painting in which the sum of the different brush strokes tells a story of how the mix of computers, techno-scientific notions and design issues has redefined the way we think of architecture in the era of information.

In guise of conclusion, in Chapter 6, I present some final reflections about what I consider the fruitful and problematic aspects the cybernetic imagination of digital architecture. I do this through an analogy between the work of digital architects and what N. K. Hayles calls the "platonic forehand and backhand" in the work of scientists. Hayles uses this idea to describe the difference between the work, characteristic of science, consisting in inferring simplified abstractions from the complexity of the world (the platonic forehand) and the situation when this logic is inverted; that is, when the abstraction appears as a substitute for the original phenomenon (the platonic backhand). Following Hayles, I use the concepts of "platonic forehand and backhand" to describe the frequent oscillation, in practices of computational architecture, between the imagination of design in reference to techno-scientific notions, and the construction of architectural issues as reifications of such resources. In this way I identify some controversial aspects of digital architecture, mainly related to the scientism common to many investigations in this field. But at the same time, I recognize possible scenarios for a meaningful cybernetic practice of architecture that is not necessarily trapped into technocratic and reified visions of architectural problems.

Notes

1 Kolarevic, *Architecture in the Digital Age.*
2 Picon, *Digital Culture in Architecture.*
3 Interestingly, the modes of analysis proposed by these authors adopt the cybernetic conception of things (as feedback systems) to explain social and cultural phenomena. In consequence, they stand as an instance of the above-mentioned expansion of cybernetic thinking in contemporary knowledge – of which the development of a computational perspective in architecture is one among many examples.
4 Latour, *Nous n'avons jamais etes modernes.*
5 Hayles, *How We Became Posthuman.*
6 Haraway, "A Cyborg Manifesto," 524.
7 Ibid., 524.
8 Takehiko & Tibbits, "ACADIA 2017 Introduction."
9 Rivka Oxman, "Thinking difference".
10 Ibid.
11 See in this respect: Breton, *Une histoire de l'informatique.*
12 The study of cybernetics is also quite useful to understand the conception of the evolution of knowledge as a feedback process between the world of technique and the world of ideas proposed by Latour, Hayles and Haraway. This framework is rich in examples of how a technical development can trigger the development of a conceptual field and vice-versa.

13 This is a key question because according to the mode of analysis of the relations between the construction of artifacts and concepts, the development of the computer is not only the product of technical advances but also of ideological considerations. Such ideological considerations are embodied by cybernetic thinking. I will come back later to this question.
14 See in this respect: Edwards, *The closed world.*
15 The Manhattan Project was the code name of the research project that lead to the production of the first atomic bomb.
16 Also known as the "Cybernetics conferences," the Macy Conferences were a series of scientific meetings held between 1946 and 1953. Organized by the Josiah Macy Jr. Foundation and chaired by Warren McCulloch, these conferences are considered a milestone in the history of cybernetics. The aim of the conferences was to set the ground of a general science dealing with the functioning of the mind, and they were the set for the exchange among a series of scientists interested in the research problems of systems theory, cybernetics, and cognitive science. See in this respect: Von Foerster et al., *Cybernetics | Kybernetik The Macy-Conferences 1946–1953.*
17 See in this respect: Heims, *Constructing a Social Science for Postwar America* and Hayles, *How We Became Posthuman.*
18 See in this respect : Breton, *Une histoire de l'informatique.*
19 All accounts of what different scholars (Castells, Lyotard, Mattelart, McLuhan) have called "network society," "informational paradigm," "information revolution, "communications society," go through the explanation of the central role of cybernetic thinking in the emergence of what, in focauldian terms, can be defined as the information episteme.
20 Hayles, *How We Became Posthuman.*
21 Joslyn & Francis Heylighen, "Cybernetics," 473
22 Ibid.
23 Wiener, *Cybernetics.*
24 See in this respect: Gallison, "The Ontology of the enemy."
25 Rosenblueth et al., "Behavior, purpose and teleology," 22.
26 The cybernetic framework has been connected to (or held responsible for) the advent of the post-modern condition (Lyotard), the emergence of a communicational paradigm (Breton), the dismantlement of the liberal subject and the rise of the post-human (Hayles), and, in general, to the evolution of the ensemble of social and natural sciences from the second half of 20th century (Lafontaine).
27 Wiener, *Cybernetics.*
28 Wiener, *The human use of human beings, 15.*
29 Ibid., 12.
30 Ibid., 21.
31 Ibid., 18.
32 Galison, "War against the center," 5-33.
33 Breton, *L'utopie de la communication.*
34 Bowker, "How to be universal."
35 Ibid., 111.
36 Ibid., 113.
37 Ibid., 116.
38 Ibid., 116.
39 Ibid., 122.
40 In this sense, it does not really matter what came first, the construction of buildings as systems or the attempt to use computers in design. What is important is to note that, just like cybernetic thinking and informatics, the technical and the ideological base of digital architecture have been inseparable.

41 See in this respect: Picon, *Digital culture in architecture.*
42 See in this respect: Rocha, *Architecture theory, 1960-1980;* Keller, *Systems Aesthetics;* Cardoso, *Builders of the Vision.*
43 Manovich, *The language of New Media.* See also: Murray, "Inventing the Medium."
44 Oxman, "Theory and design in the first digital age," 262.
45 Hayles, *How we Became Posthuman,* 15.

Bibliography

Breton, Philippe. *L'utopie de la Communication: Le Mythe du Village Planetaire.* Paris: La decouverte, 1995.

—. *Une Histoire De l'informatique.* Paris: La decouverte, 1990.

Bowker, Geof. "How to Be Universal: Some Cybernetic Strategies, 1943-70." *Social Studies of Science* 23, no. 1 (1993).

Cardoso, Daniel. *Builders of the Vision. Software and the Imagination of Design.* New York, NY: Routledge, 2015.

Edwards, Paul N.. *The Closed World. Computers and the Politics of Discourse in Cold War America.* Cambridge, MA: The MIT Press, 1997.

Gallison, Peter. "War Against the Center." In *Architecture and the Sciences: Exchanging Metaphors.* Edited by Antoine Picon and Alessandra Ponte, 196–227. Princeton, New Jersey: Princeton Architectural Press, 2003.

Haraway, Donna. "A Cyborg Manifesto. Science, Technology, and Socialist Feminism in the Late Twentieth Century." In *The New Media Reader.* Edited by Noah Wardrip-Fruin and Nick Montfort, 515–541. Cambridge, Londres: The MIT Press, 2003.

Hayles, N. Katherine. *How We Became Posthuman: Virtual Bodies in Cybernetics, Literature and Informatics.* Chicago: The University of Chicago Press, 1999.

Heims, Steve J.. *Consnstructing a Social Science for Postwar America. The Cybernetics Group, 1946-1953.* Cambridge, MA: The MIT Press, 1993.

Joslyn, Cliff, and Francis Heylighen. "Cybernetics." *Encyclopedia of Computer Science.* 2003. 470–473.

Keller, Sean. *Systems Aesthetics: Architectural Theory at the University of Cambridge, 1960-1975. Doctotral Dissertation.* Cambridge, MA: Harvard University, 2005.

Kolarevic, Branco. *Architecture in the Digital Age. Design and Manufacturing.* New York, Londres: Spon Press, 2003.

Latour, Bruno. *Nous n'avons Jamais été Modernes: Essai d'anthropologie Symétrique.* Paris: La decouverte, 1992.

Manovich, Lev. *The Language of New Media.* Cambridge, Mass: The MIT Press, 2001.

Murray, Janet H.. "Inventing the Medium." In *The New Media Reader.* Edited by Noah Wardrip-Fruin and Nick Montfort, 3–11. Cambridge, Londres: The MIT Press, 2003.

Oxman, Rivka. "Thinking Difference: Theories and Models of Parametric Design Thinking." *Design Studies* 52 (2017): 4–39.

—. "Theory and Design in the First Digital Age." *Design Studies* 27 (2006): 229–65.

Picon, Antoine. *Digital Culture in Architecture. An Introduction for the Design Professions.* Basel: Birkhauser GMBH, 2010.

Rocha, AltinoJoao, and Magalhaes. *Architecture Theory 1960- 1980. Emergence of a Computational Perspective. Doctoral Dissertation.* Cambridge, MA: Massachusetts Institute of Technology, 2004.

Takehiko, Nagakura, and Skylar Tibbits. "ACADIA." *ACADIA 2017 Introduction. Disciplines & Disruption.* 2017. http://2017.acadia.org (accessed December 1, 2017).

Von Foerster, Heinz, John Stroud, S Kubie Lawrence, and Norbert Wiener. *Cybernetics| Kybernetik The Macy-Conferences 1946–1953.* Edited by Claus Pias. Zurich/Berlin: Diaphanes, 2003.

Wiener, Norbert. *Cybernetics or Control and Communication in the Animal and the Machine.* Cambridge, MA: The MIT Press, 1961.

—. *The Human Use of Human Beings: Cybernetics and Society.* London: Free Association Books, 1989.

2 Cybernetics and the architecture of performance

Besides the use of the computer as a preferred means of production, most digital architecture practices share another common feature, they usually construct architectural objects as dynamic devices, as self-regulated artifacts, as responsive objects and as sorts of semi-organic machines. These visions of architectural objects have been elaborated since the 1960s in reference to a series of discourses, still in force today, about the performance of architecture. As we will see below, the concept of performance holds the key to understand the evolution of the computational perspective in architecture not only as a technical event determined by the logic of the computer, but as a reinterpretation of the problems of the profession according to an informational conception of things. As a matter of fact, the notion of performance, as it is commonly used in digital architecture practices, evokes an informational conception of the built environment. In the work of digital architects the idea of performance is directly connected to a vision of architectural objects informed by the cybernetic framework, which, as discussed in the previous sections, promoted a conception of things in the world as systems of interrelated phenomena and as entities immersed in permanent processes of information exchange.

Said the above, it is important to clarify that in architecture the notion of performance did not arrive exclusively via information discourses. According to Michael Hensel, the concept of performance in architecture has been shaped by a series of historical factors that include the influence of various scientific developments on architecture from the mid eighteenth century. Among the factors that shaped this notion are the emergence of the notions of *environment*, *milieu,* and *Umwelt*, as described in the writings of Auguste Compte and Jakob von Uexkull, and in the twentieth century, the rise of the *performative turn* movement and systems theory.[1]

The previously mentioned developments allowed the emergence of new conceptions of human culture, of artistic production and of scientific practice which, in general terms, are grounded on the idea that different things in the world (human behavior, artistic productions, natural phenomena) are performed actions that affect and are affected by a specific context. From this perspective, in the humanities and social sciences culture at large

DOI: 10.4324/9781003181101-2

started to be considered as performance. In the arts, the performative view replaced the conception of artistic productions as works by its conception as events that involve the spectator and that engage spatial and temporal aspects. In scientific practice, the idea of performance enabled a shift from its conception as a "representational idiom" to a "performative idiom"; that is, as a practice that effects relations among various cultural elements and that operates the production of knowledge as a way of doing things.[2]

In architectural practice, the *performative turn* allowed the rise of diverse approaches towards the question of performance. Hensel identifies four dominant approaches. The first approach is connected to an interest in representation, symbolism, and meaning. Exemplified by Charles Jenks' "Radical Eclecticism," this approach aimed to mobilize different kinds of meaning which appealed to different capacities of the mind and of the body. The second and third approaches reenact the debates about the relationship between form and function, and they can be divided into formal and functional takes on performance. Finally, the fourth approach focuses in the construction of architecture as an event, which mobilizes conceptions of the built environment as an occurrence and as the lieu for the emergence of the unplanned.[3]

As it will be seen later, digital architecture practices are connected in different ways to the abovementioned approaches, particularly with the formal, functional, and (what might be called) "eventmental" approaches. As a matter of fact, the development of digital architecture has been closely connected to these explorations. According to my analysis, the main lesson that digital architects learned from the *performative turn* is that things in the world are performed actions that affect and are affected by a specific context.[4] Indeed, this idea underlies the abovementioned performative approaches which, ultimately, lie beneath one of the most common tropes of digital architecture: the idea that buildings are performative objects that act in the world and upon which the world acts. It is in this sense that can be established a connection between the *performative turn* in digital architecture and the cybernetic paradigm.

According to the cybernetic view, things in the world cannot be conceived as individual entities. On the contrary, from a cybernetic perspective, phenomena must be considered as a combination of interconnected elements, as constitutive parts of bigger systems. Importantly, in cybernetic theory the notion of performance is inherent to the conception of phenomena according to the abovementioned relational logic. As a matter of fact, the concept of performance is central to the study of the behavior of systems (either machines or living beings) in terms of relations. As it was discussed earlier, in cybernetic theory to think of the behavior of systems in terms of a relational logic is to think of the exchange of information that they establish with their surrounding environment. In cybernetic thinking, the concept of performance describes how well a system solves these exchanges. More precisely, the performance of a system is a measure of these exchanges. For Wiener, for example, the structure of an organism, or of a servomechanism, is an indicator of the performance that can be expected from it. In this respect, Aaron Sprecher explains that "the way information is organized, dispersed, and translated regulates the performative aspects of an organism in regards to its environment."[5] In other words, in cybernetic thinking the performance of a system is the measure of its capacity to adapt and respond to a given context.

Following the cybernetic acceptation of the concept of performance, in contemporary architectural thinking this notion describes an approach to architectural design grounded on the idea that buildings perform on a specific environment that, inversely, performs on them. This idea is central to several design methodologies based on the analysis of the suitability of a given design solution according to the conditions and requirements of a given design problem. As expressed by architect and digital design researcher Yehuda E. Kalay, the question of the performance of architecture has been oriented, "to assess the desirability of the behavior of the confluence of the form, function and context."[6] From this statement it follows that, from a performative view, buildings are interconnected systems that cannot be conceived as independent from the context in which they exist. This rather simple idea represents a radical paradigm shift in architectural thinking that is at the core of the development of digital architecture.

In order to illustrate the significance of the informational view of things for the abovementioned transformation, in the following pages I will trace the cybernetic ascendancy of the performative conception of architecture. To do so I will visit different definitions of the concept of performance in architecture, and I will discuss the role of cybernetic thinking in *Performance Design*, a seminal computer-based design model presented in 1967 by the journal *Progressive Architecture*. This survey will permit me to show how, by embracing the discourses of performance, several contemporary practices of digital architecture have promoted a cybernetic imagination of design issues. Thereby, I will also explain the relationship between the performative conception of architecture and the technological base of computational design. Finally, I will discuss the connection between the notion of performance and the conceptions of architectural space and of the inhabitant inherent to the work of digital architects.

Through this analysis, I aim to show to what extent the key themes of digital architecture can be traced back to the early research of computing in design, which was inseparable from the conceptualization of buildings as performative devices, that is, as objects involved in a process of information exchange with their surrounding environment.

The performative turn in digital architecture

It is interesting to observe that the origin of the previously described performative approach in architectural practice coincided with the early use of computers in the profession – which at the dawn of digital architecture were mainly employed to systematize quantitative aspects of a design problem such as the estimated construction costs and structural analyses. The reason why I find this connection meaningful is that, as we will see, it shows that from the moment when architects started to use computers to solve design problems, they started to think of architectural issues in terms of the ontology of information fostered by cybernetic theory.

As mentioned before, since the 1960s, the notion of performance has been associated in digital architecture to the development of a series of (functional, formal, and eventmental) design approaches oriented to the optimization of the architectural object, the study of the material behavior of buildings, the exploration of aesthetic inscriptions of performance, as well as the characterization of architectural objects as dynamic, generative and autonomous systems.[7] Despite these differences in approach, in general terms, the performative explorations of digital architecture describe a practice of design based on the integration into architectural problems (largely thanks to the development of digital design and simulation tools) of a variety of programmatic and contextual aspects (which include environmental factors and material characteristics of the building, as well as social, cultural, ecological, aesthetic, and technological perspectives).

I identify two main tendencies among the performative approaches in digital architecture. On the one hand, there are the explorations that have investigated the idea of performance in relation to the functional and technical aspects of buildings. On the other hand, there are the investigations oriented to the interpretation of the performance of architecture in relation to the sensorial and symbolic aspects of the built space. While, in the first case, the notion of performance has been considered a question of accomplishing an intended purpose under a set of given conditions, in the second case, the performance of architecture has been chiefly associated to the consideration of buildings as events and as mediation devices between the users and the environment (a condition that digital architects have deeply explored both in aesthetical and practical terms).

Concerning the technical and functional aspects of architecture, the discourses of performance-based architecture have fostered a vision of design as a problem of optimization and efficiency. Such pragmatic conception of design can be observed in the early practices of computer-based architecture, which, as it will be discussed later, developed in direct reference to the fields of operations research and systems analysis; that is, they considered design as a problem-solving question. In this sense, it was assumed that the best answer to an architectural problem was the fastest, the most profitable and efficient. From this perspective, performance-based design has been considered as a means of responding accurately to the different aspects of an architectural project, such as the structural behavior of the building, the proper functioning of its conditioning systems, and other factors related to energy consumption and building comfort. But, more importantly, in this way architectural objects have been considered as integrated wholes, as systems resulting from the interconnection among a set of functions, elements, and subsystems, whose adequate connections guaranty the proper functioning of the building as a whole.

The corollary of the holistic conception of architecture has been the construction of buildings as forms of organization that respond to a given context that is composed by a multiplicity of actors, factors and forces.[8] At this point, the functional approaches and the "eventmental" approaches meet on common ground, because they both imply to consider the building as the outcome of the conditions of a given context (be them defined by the weather or the perceptions of the users of the built space). This is possibly the fundamental aspect of the performative conception of architecture. From this perspective, performance-based design models have explored visions of the built environment as a problem of varied and dynamic relations, where building systems are conceived as element into a vast network of factors that define a spatial reality – an idea that was central to Frederick Kiesler's research, presented in the seminal article *On Correalism and Biotechnique.*[9]

In contemporary architectural thinking, the abovementioned conception of architectural issues has been at the core of a professional praxis in which the notion of performance stands for a conception of design as the search of the proper balance between the designed object and the context. Such ontology of the architectural object was shared by various architects and design theorists (among them Christopher Alexander, John Frazer, and Lionel March) who, at the dawn of digital architecture, investigated conceptions of design as a problem solving question involving varied and dynamic relations. As a result of these conceptions of design consolidated a new imagination of architecture – that emerged hand in hand with the introduction of information technology in the profession – which conceives of buildings as the product of an active process that reflects the complex relations among the architectural object and the different factors and forces that define a given design problem. Over the years, this conception of the disciplinary problems has been shared by several influential practitioners of digital architecture; in many investigations of digital design, buildings are considered as the outcome of feedback systems that involve numerous factors.

In such explorations, the use of computer-based design methodologies has far exceeded the functional approaches oriented to problems of efficiency and optimization. It has been a means to experiment with ideas about the kinetic and generative in design, about the notions of effect and affect in contemporary architecture, and about the perception and cognition of space. In this respect, the broad panorama of digital architecture presented by Antoine Picon in *Digital Culture in Architecture* is particularly illuminating. Picon's study shows that the explorations of digital architecture concerned with performative conceptions of design issues have been so prolific that it is likely to claim that most computer-based design practices can be defined in one way or another in relation to the concept of performance.[10] More importantly, despite the diversity of approaches and goals of digital design investigations, the conception of architectural objects underlying them is essentially the same. It is a vision that fosters a comprehension of architectural issues according to a relational logic. It is a logic that implies thinking of buildings as the result of the complex interaction among the various aspects involved in the definition of a spatial reality. Evidently, this way of thinking about architecture is directly connected to the cybernetic model of causality. The paradigmatic example of the early connection between digital design and the cybernetic imagination of architectural issues is *Performance Design*. This model represents a seminal approach to computer-based design which, according to William Braham, was inspired by the early work of pioneers of cybernetic architecture such as Christopher Alexander, Peter McCleary, and Lionel March and involved a re-conceptualization of architectural problems in relation to information discourses and techniques.

The cybernetics of performance design

Performance Design was presented in a 1967 volume of *Progressive Architecture*. The model was described as a set of practices that intended to explore the possibilities offered to the disciplines of architecture and urban design by scientific fields such as systems analysis and operations research. According to the editors, these fields of knowledge permit to see a series of isolated objects as interconnected and mutually dependent elements.[11] Accordingly, by promoting a conception of the built space based on the concepts and techniques of these models, *Performance Design* promoted both the construction of architecture and the city as systems of interrelated elements and a systemic mode of analysis to study buildings and the urban space from a holistic perspective. On the basis of these proposals was the idea that buildings and the urban space can be described as the set of relations among the diverse elements that participate in their definition.

According to the cybernetic definition of performance, the model posited that the measure of success of a given solution to a given design problem is the behavior, or the performance, of the designed object. In other words, performance is defined as the indicator to estimate the adequate, or inadequate, fit among the different elements that compose the designed system.

At this point, it is possible to observe the patent connection between the design approach fostered by *Performance Design* and the "utility function" central to the logic of the "optimization methods" exposed by Herbert Simon in *The Sciences of the Artificial*.[12] For Simon, an artifact is the meeting point (the interface) between its internal environment (the artifact's organization) and a given external environment (the context in which the artifact operates). In concordance with this description of designed

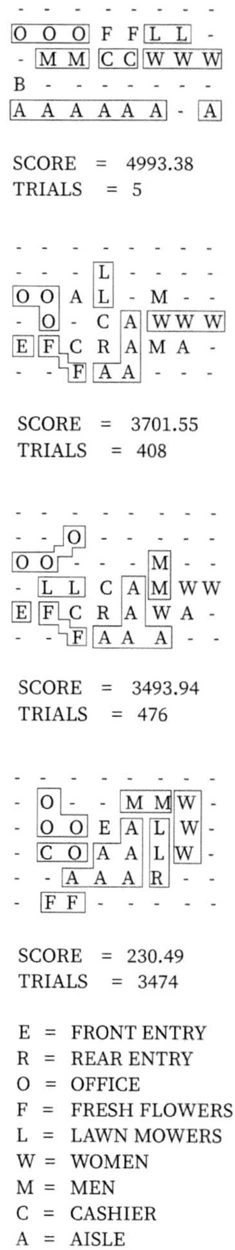
- - - - - - - - -
O O O F F L L -
- M M C C W W W
B - - - - - - - -
A A A A A A - A
SCORE = 4993.38
TRIALS = 5
- - - - - - - - -
- - - L - - - -
O O A L - M - -
- O - C A W W W
E F C R A M A -
- - F A A - - -
SCORE = 3701.55
TRIALS = 408
- - - - - - - - -
- - O - - - - -
O O - - - M - -
- L L C A M W W
E F C R A W A -
- - F A A A - -
SCORE = 3493.94
TRIALS = 476
- - - - - - - - -
- O - - M M W -
- O O E A L W -
- C O A A L W -
- - A A A R - -
- F F - - - - -
SCORE = 230.49
TRIALS = 3474
E = FRONT ENTRY
R = REAR ENTRY
O = OFFICE
F = FRESH FLOWERS
L = LAWN MOWERS
W = WOMEN
M = MEN
C = CASHIER
A = AISLE

Figure 2.1

objects (the artificial), Simon describes the logic of optimization methods as follows:

> The *inner environment of* the design problem is represented by a set of given alternatives of action. The alternatives may be given *in extenso*: more commonly they are specified in terms of command variables that have defined domains. The *outer environment* is represented by a set of parameters, which may be known with certainty or only in terms of a probability distribution. The goals for adaptation of inner to outer environment are defined by a utility function, usually scalar, of the command variables and environmental parameters perhaps supplemented by a number of constraints (inequalities, say, between functions of the command variables and environmental parameters).[13]

Following this logic, *Performance Design* was described in *Progressive Architecture* as a process consisting of four phases. The first phase consists of the definition of the design problem. The second phase comprises the definition of the requirements of the system – this includes the quantification of all the aspects of the system, or, for the non-quantifiable aspects, the development of experiments that allow the designer to predict their behavior. In the third phase the system is separated into its parts, components, and subsystems. The purpose of this phase is the comprehension of the influence of the characteristics of each part and their effect in the global performance of the system. Finally, the fourth phase corresponds to the implementation of the conclusions reached. This last phase includes a feedback process in which the real performance of the designed object is compared to the planned performance. This process permits to fix the failures of the system and test the impact of the possible corrections into the implemented design solutions.

The above description of the design process as advanced by *Performance Design* is clearly related to two ideas, central to Simon's influential work. Crucially, such ideas were inherent to the development of computer science and are still considered valid today. I refer, on the one hand, to the belief that a great amount of things can be quantified to be systematically analyzed. On the other hand, I refer to the conviction that information technology is the ideal tool to solve any kind of problem, especially those problems that include many variables due to their complexity. Accordingly, *Performance Design* fostered an epistemology of design grounded on the processing of data and variables corresponding to the diverse factors that participate in the definition of an architectural reality.

The aforementioned epistemology of design illustrates clearly that, along with the use of computational technology, the influence of cybernetic thinking was fundamental for the construction of the performative view in digital architecture. Summarizing, such influence is particularly evident in three central aspects of the design approach advanced by *Performance*

Design. First, the consideration of built spaces as systems. Second, the proposal to analyze designs according to their behavior. Third, the use of information as the regulatory factor of design and as a tool to measure the performance of the designed object. As a matter of fact, the influence of cybernetic thinking in *Performance Design* was evident for the editors of *Progressive Architecture*, who claimed that the fields of knowledge that inspired the model were part of the technological and scientific base developed as part of the war efforts made by the United Sates and the United Kingdom during World War Two – a period of intense scientific research from which the cybernetic revolution gained momentum.[14] With this claim, the promoters of the model overtly situated *Performance Design* into the ensemble of developments connected to the cybernetic paradigm.[15]

According to the above, the model of *Performance Design* exemplifies the close relationship that has existed, in digital architecture practices, between the definition of new design agendas grounded on the use of information technology and the redefinition of architectural issues in reference to the informational paradigm. In this sense, this model stands out as a paradigmatic example of what I am trying to demonstrate in this book. I refer to the fact that the changes of the profession embodied in the productions of digital architecture are not only the product of the introduction of computer-based modes of production in architectural practice, but of the construction of an imagination of design grounded on the ideas put into circulation by cybernetic thinking. These ideas have migrated from cybernetic theory to a variety of scientific fields and theories, whose ideas have been adopted by digital architects as a means to re-conceptualize architectural problems. In these re-conceptualization processes, information technology and information discourse become inseparable.

As an instance of the former assertion, take the case of the design method described by *Performance Design*. In this example, the idea of interpreting architectural problems as a question of integration among the building and the environment was inseparable from the modes of production of informatics: manipulation of formal systems, quantification, mathematical expression, etc. Yet, as we have seen, although the pragmatics of computers were a central feature of the proposed design model, the imagination of design inherent to this model expresses, above the technical aspects of computing, an informational ontology of architecture. The above applies to several explorations of digital architecture that, by means of the performative conception of the built environment, have endorsed a cybernetic imagination of design issues.

The performativity of digital architecture

The abovementioned connection between the performative view and the cybernetic construction of design issues is a central element of many contemporary explorations of digital architecture. In such explorations, it is not uncommon to discern constructions of design and architectural objects that call to mind the cybernetic narratives about the communicational nature of organisms and machines, as well as other ideas inherited from the cybernetic framework. Among the informational narratives that inform digital architecture, perhaps the most common are the allusions to the cybernetic logic of circular causality and to the role of information as a regulatory force of the design process. From the cybernetic perspective, these two ideas are inseparable. The logic of circular causality implies the exchange of information, which in cybernetic thinking is the regulatory element that guarantees that any system achieves a point of equilibrium with its environment. So, when digital architects describe architectural design as an information-centered practice grounded upon the manipulation of data, they do not refer only (or particularly) to the modes of production of informatics. Beyond the technical aspects of digital design, this idea describes a new ontology of the architectural object. In reference to the conception of architecture as an information-driven practice, digital architects have re-inscribed in architectural terms a series of cybernetic themes. For instance, they have described buildings as sorts of feedback systems, as homeostatic mechanisms, and as teleological objects able to achieve a state of equilibrium thanks to the permanent exchange between the architectural object and its context.

This shift in architectural thinking can be observed in numerous contemporary practices of performance-based digital design. Take, for instance, a design research by Christopher Hight, described in the article *High-performance anxiety*.[16] In the cited paper, Hight presents a design research based on the use of what he calls "the computational paradigms of performance."[17] Interestingly, when he describes such paradigms, he does it in direct reference to well-known cybernetic idioms. For example, Hight describes the produced designs as systems which operate "within informational flows as Maxwell's demons momentarily reversing entropic probabilities" and as emergent solutions that develop "geometry, spatial and formal coherence immanent to the diverse forces that flow across the site."[18]

The above narrative of a performance-based design process resonates clearly with the writings of Norbert Wiener, as the reference to the three essential topics of cybernetics (information, organization, and entropy) is evident. Here information (or negative entropy in cybernetic terms), the regulatory mechanism that enables a system to keep a state of equilibrium, is employed to define design as a process based on the feedback among the analysis of the known data about a given problem and a set of possible solutions. In this way, the project explores a logic of design in which the resulting project emerges as a form of organization (as opposed to entropy) that embodies the forces that shape it, and that promises "a design that approaches figuration (but not a figure) that constructs different ecologies amidst the social, natural and subjective worlds."[19]

Interestingly, in the example presented by Hight, the use of information as the regulatory element of design implies the conception of the built space as an ecology, as an artifact that is in the middle of social, natural and subjective realms. In the work of some of the most influential practitioners of digital architecture, who have endorsed a notion of performance associated to an operative conception of design and of designed objects, appear the same questions; namely, the connection between the construction of design as an information-driven practice and the conception of the built environment as what emerges from the forces present in a given context, and of course, the description of design issues in reference to cybernetic concepts.

For instance, when Lars Spuybroek describes a design methodology that he calls "intensive design techniques," he alludes to different cybernetic ideas that are directly connected to the conception of design as an informational process. In this respect, Spuybroek argues that, "To map inward going and outward going forces, and to map contractive and expansive forces within one continuum, a networked self-organizing technique is required. An intensive design technique means to inform a virtual system, which, during the processing of that information, takes on an actual structure that is a registering of the information."[20] In the method advanced by the director of NOX, design is conceived as a process based on a computational logic that involves the analysis of inputs and outputs. The corollary of this informational conception of design is the construction of the built environment as embodied information; in the intensive design technique advanced by Spuybroek, architecture appears as the result of an exchange of information that materializes in architectural form.

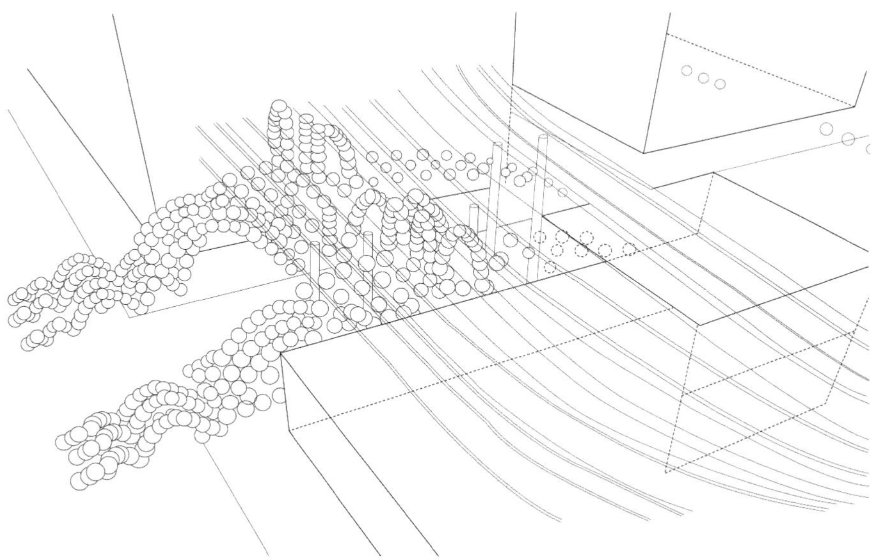

Figure 2.2

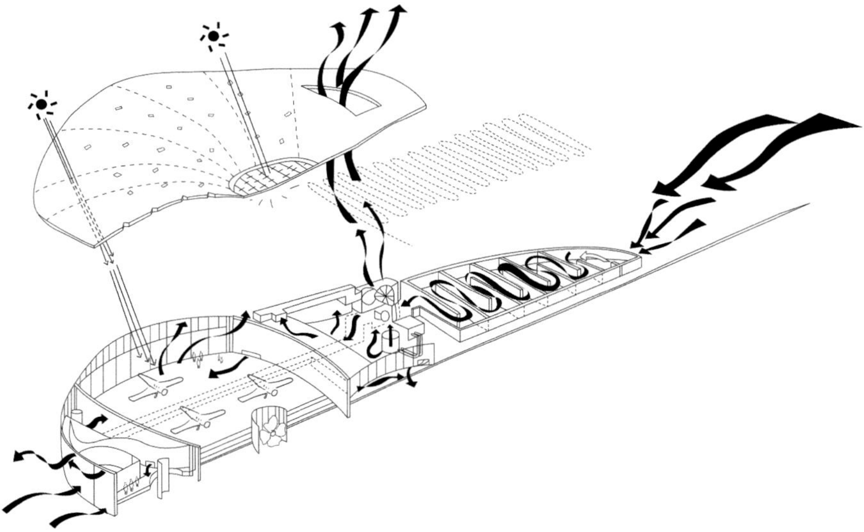

Figure 2.3

A very similar conception of architectural design is presented by Greg Lynn in his popular essay *Animate Form*. In the mentioned essay, Lynn describes an information-driven practice of architecture in which, thanks to the use of animation software, the form of the building is produced as the actualization of the forces that take part in its definition. Thereby, Lynn imagines a series of design scenarios where "the context for design becomes an active abstract space that directs form within a current of forces that can be stored as information in the shape of the form."[21] Once again, architecture is described as the result of flows of information embodied in architectural form, as a performed action that, in accordance with the conception of things inherent to the *performative turn*, is affected by a specific context.

In a certain way, these are the same ideas that are at the core of the diagrammatic work of architectural studios such as UN Studio and Foreign Office Architects. Ben van Berkel and Caroline Bos, for instance, have referred to their work with diagrams as a technique to think of design as a practice mediated by information flows.[22] Accordingly, in the diagrammatic work of UN Studio, the information collected about a given design problem is mapped as a visual representation that works at the same time as an analytic tool and as a formal scheme that supports the design process. In like manner, Alejandro Zaera Polo has discussed computer mediated design as a way of introducing and visualizing information corresponding to a series of aspects external to the building, such as time, light, temperature, and weight, and as a means to use these data as inputs of the design process.[23]

The above examples are paradigmatic of the conception of design as a feedback system that involves the building and the environment. This idea,

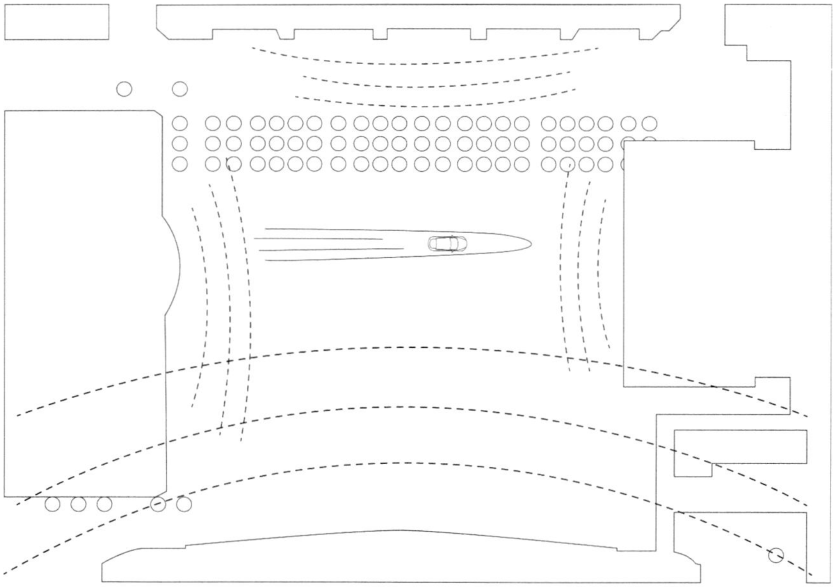

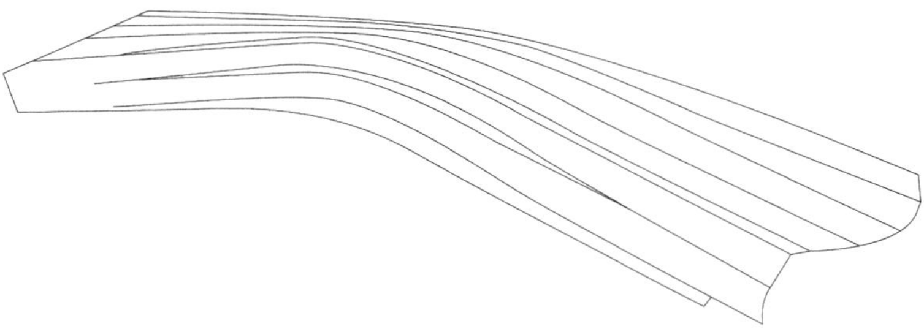

Figure 2.4

advanced by the promoters of *Performance Design* back in the 1960s, has been systematically employed to think of the interrelation among the architectural object and the context. The emblematic example of this cybernetic conception of the relation between architecture and environment is the design methodology proposed by Christopher Alexander in his prominent essay *Notes on the Synthesis of Form*,[24] which endorses a performative conception of design issues grounded on the inseparability of architecture and environment. As a matter of fact, for Alexander, to design an object is to affect the environment on which such object performs. For instance, he claims that "the environment must be organized so that its own regeneration and construction does not constantly disrupt its performance."[25] Accordingly, the starting point of the design method proposed by Alexander is to consider architectural form as the result of the correct fit among of the requirements of a design project and the conditions of a given context. In this regard, Alexander notes that, "when we speak of design, the real object of discussion is not the form alone, but the ensemble comprising the form and its context. Good fit is a desired property of this ensemble which relates to some particular division of the ensemble into form and context."[26]

More recently Ali Rahim has described the question of the performance of architecture practically in the same terms. According to Rahim, the notion of performance in architecture refers to the material, organizational and cultural change resulting from an emergent process that includes feedback loops among the diverse actors and factors that participate in the materialization of the built environment. From this perspective, Rahim conceives the creation of architectural form as a process determined by the reaction to external stimuli which transforms a "habitational situation." The former would be the result of feedback loops between both a subject and the environment, and between architecture and the context. In Rahim's projects, this idea is inherent to a design logic where the architectural form is conceived as a reactive system, as a "catalytic formation" that responds to stimuli and which is immersed into a network of elements which include the material aspects of architecture, the environment, and its inhabitants.[27]

Performative tools, buildings, and users

According to my proposal of considering the evolution of digital architecture as a seriation (that is, as a field in which the technical aspects and the conceptual fields evolve together in a process of circular causality), the creation of computer-based approaches to design is not the cause but the corollary of the construction of an informational imagination of architecture. From this perspective, it is understood that the use of information technology in architecture was motivated by the construction of architectural issues in reference to the frameworks that appeared hand in hand with the emergence of computer science. In the same way, it is assumed that, inversely, the exploration of computer-based design methods also encouraged the construction of informational explanations of architecture. This circular logic is not only in the origin of performative modes of production of space (design tools and methods) resulting from the use of computers in architectural practice. As will be seen below, the performative view, which was inherent to the development of early digital design approaches, is also at the core of conceptions of space, of the inhabitant and even of the role of architects promoted by the practitioners of digital architecture.

Regarding the connection between the performative view and the development of digital design tools, consider how the modes of production of architecture allowed by computational design methods are closely connected to the above-mentioned imagination of architectural objects as self-regulated, responsive, interconnected devices. For instance, if one looks at the design logic inherent to the dominant models of computer-based design, as described by Rivka Oxman in her article *Theory and design in the first digital age,* it seems clear that the relational logic fostered by the performative/cybernetic conception of architecture has been at the core of the development of the technological base of digital design.

Oxman classifies digital design models in five main categories (CAD models, digital formation models, generative design models, performance-based formation models, and integrated compound models) and nine subcategories (CAD descriptive models, generation-evaluation CAD models, topological formation models, associative design formation models, motion-based formation models, grammatical transformative design models, evolutionary design models, and performance-based generation models).[28]

Interestingly, according to the above taxonomy of digital design approaches, the evolution of these models tends towards the definition of performance-based design approaches. The former comes as no surprise since, according to Oxman, what differentiates these computer-based design models from traditional design practices is the possibility of establishing multi-directional connections among the various aspects of a design process (generation, representation, evaluation, and performance evaluation of the designed form). Despite the technical and conceptual differences between the various models described in *Theory and design in the first digital age*, they all share a common feature. All of them allow the designer to interact, to a greater or lesser extent, with the designed object at different stages of the design process, to analyze different design scenarios according to diverse variables, and to feedback the design process with the results of the corresponding analyses. In other words, they all embody a design logic that expresses a central question explored by the promoters of *Performance Design* that ever since has been at the core of the investigations of digital architects. Namely, the conception of the built environment as the result of various interconnected and mutually dependent elements and of architectural design as a means to resolve adequately the relations among such elements.

The former is the main idea behind the development of a series of design techniques and methods which, thanks to the use of the computer, have allowed designers to define dynamic procedures to produce the architectural form, to include data flows as inputs of the design process, to explore new formal vocabularies that evoke new conceptions of space, to automate different aspects of the design process through the use of algorithmic techniques and, more recently, to inform the design process with the analysis of the material behavior of the designed object. From the creation of the Sketchpad to the development of the most recent software of parametric design, the advances of digital design technology have expressed conceptions of architectural space that can be connected to the visions of things inherent to the performative turn in architecture.

The same can be said about the spatial explorations, associated to the use of the computers in design, advanced by digital architects. Naturally, the performative view of architecture underlying the discourses and the techniques of digital design is also reflected in the forms and spaces projected by digital architects. Some critics and theorists have claimed that the use of digital design tools in architecture has been largely motivated by the possibilities that these tools offer to produce and control complex geometries, very difficult to draw with traditional drafting tools. As a matter of fact, the investigation of new formal typologies has been a central aspect of the work of digital architects, and one of the most visible results of the research in this field has been the emergence of an entire new formal repertoire in the contemporary architectural landscape. Yet, it is important to note that in the practice of many digital designers the production of complex form has not always been an end in itself.[29] On the contrary, the formal explorations of digital architects have been frequently connected to the new theoretical frameworks that emerged hand in hand with the first explorations of information technology in the profession. In this respect, Oxman recalls that along with the exploration of generative, parametric, topological design techniques (inherent to the models described in *Theory and design in the first digital age*), digital architects have imagined a variety of constructions of design issues in reference to a body of scientific concepts related to the "morphology of complexity such as hyper-continuity and hyper-connectivity," the "biological conditions of networked connectivity and rhizome-like complexity," the "new complexity of non-linear, networked conditions," and different "evolutionary models of nature."[30]

As we will see in the next chapters, many of these techno-scientifically inspired constructions of design issues are architectural interpretations of a series of ideas inherited from different fields of knowledge and theories directly connected to the cybernetic paradigm, including computer science. We have seen earlier that the translation into architectural discourse of a variety of scientific concepts has been the base of the cybernetic construction of architectural objects as dynamic interconnected systems, as self-regulated objects, as semi-organic machines, etcetera. We have also seen that the conception of buildings as performative objects is directly connected to these ideas. In accordance with such narratives, the productions of digital architects feature a universe of forms that evoke the discourses that inspire them. As a matter of fact, a look at any anthology of computational design is enough to notice that the imagery of digital architecture is composed by a collection of shapes of biological inspiration that call to mind the morphology of natural systems, by complex spatial configurations that call to mind the forces that shape them, by design concepts that translate the logic of computing, and by seamless spatial typologies where the distinctions between architecture and context, inside and outside, structural and spatial

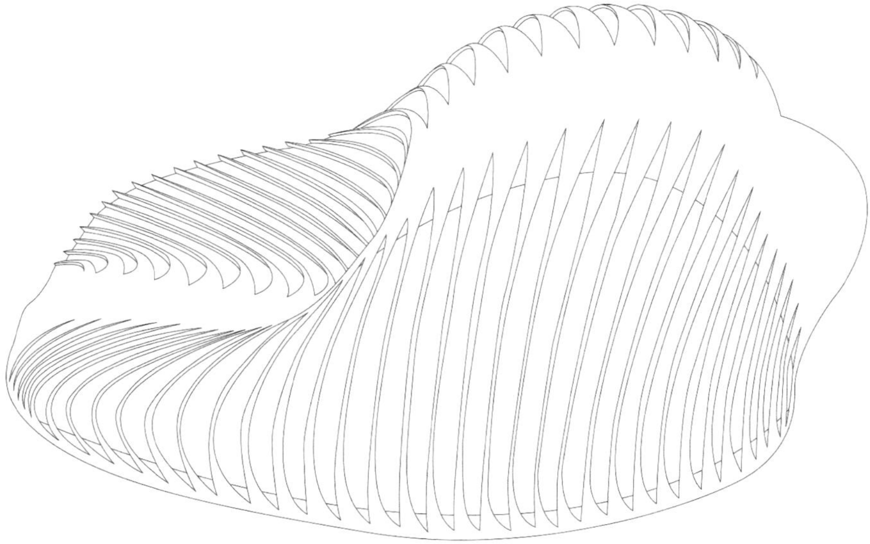

Figure 2.5

design are blurred – perhaps as a reminder of how the cybernetic paradigm blurred the boundaries among the main categories (human/animal, natural/artificial, individual/society) on which western culture (and by extension western architecture) had been grounded until the mid-twentieth century.

In this sense, it is possible to claim that the formal explorations displayed by digital designers are not just motivated by the possibility to produce complex forms. Quite often, these searches are driven by a search to accommodate the cybernetic conceptions of a new kind of architectural space; it is a kind of space which is no longer conceived as a static formation but as a complex dynamic system.

Of course, the emergence of new conceptions of architectural space also implied the construction of other ways of thinking of the relationship between buildings and inhabitants (and of inhabitants themselves). In opposition to the ideals of order, clarity and standardization fostered by mainstream modern architecture, the productions of digital architecture are more connected to post-modern values such as difference, versatility, and complexity.[31] In consequence, the buildings conceived by digital architects are no longer designed for an ideal man, nor they promote a normalized way of life. On the contrary, each project considers the particularities of its users (and, why not, their dysfunctionalities[32]) as inputs of design. Brought to the limits of paroxysm, this idea appears in many projects of digital architecture that dream of the possibility of producing adaptable buildings able to react to the moods and actions of their dwellers.

Crucially, the emergence of a user that might be called the "performative inhabitant" is not alien to some of the key transformations in contemporary thinking that different scholars have attributed to the emergence of

Figure 2.6

cybernetics. For instance, the social researcher Céline Lafontaine considers that the disappearance in contemporary social sciences of the liberal subject as the model of the free and autonomous human being is a direct consequence of a cybernetic theme; namely, the analogy between the computer and the brain fostered both by cybernetitians and computer scientists and widely accepted in contemporary western society. According to Lafontaine, the possibility of transferring to machines the ability to think implied a devaluation of reason and its dissociation from human subjectivity (two values historically considered exclusively human and a product of the human's interiority). A key idea implicit in cybernetic thinking is that individual subjectivity is not a distinctive characteristic of humans but an informational process that can be transferred to machines. As explained by Lafontaine, this idea was central to the cybernetic erasure of the frontiers between living and non-living, and it also put an end to the conception of subjectivity as a particular human feature. In this sense, she argues that the

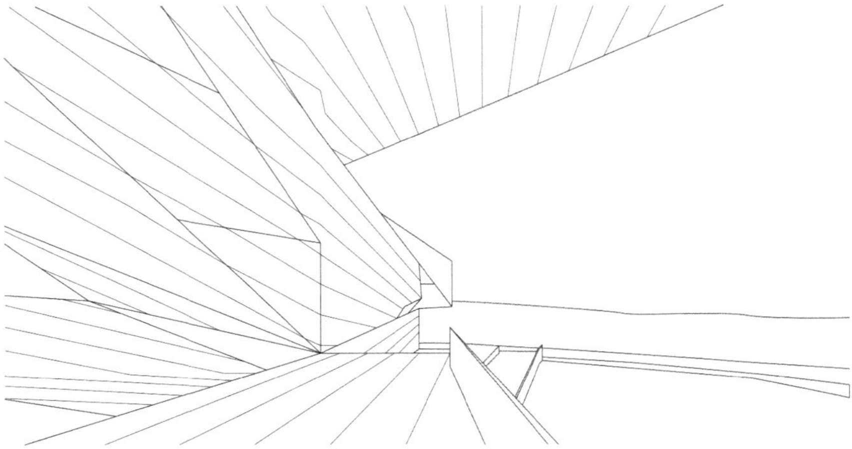

Figure 2.7

advent of cybernetics (and cybernetic technology) contributed to the exit of humanism from the modern political landscape.[33]

The sociologist of science Philippe Breton exposes a similar argument. For him, the anti-humanism of cybernetic theory resulted in an anthropological redefinition of the human being that stems from the idea that the essence of life is no longer in biology but in communication.[34] Breton explains that the cybernetic ontology considers humans as entities immersed into a continuous flux of exchanges and relations with an external world. In this regard, he reminds that, according to Wiener, to be alive is to participate in a continuous flow of influences coming from the outside world, in which humans only represent an intermediate stage. In consequence, cybernetic thinking does not consider the human being the center of everything, as in classical conceptions of mankind, but the human is considered an intermediary element among the crossed communicational processes that characterize any society.[35] Indeed, from this perspective humans are not even considered individuals anymore. This conception of humans is central to the work of the cybernetitian and anthropologist Gregory Bateson, who reimagined society in informational terms. Bateson's influential work envisions society as a kind of communicational system grounded on the interdependence of the people that form it, while the human mind is imagined as the informational process that constitutes society. Therefore, the individual, defined basically as a social being, disappears among the interpersonal determinants relative to the communication system, that is, society.[36]

In accordance with this cybernetic conception of humans, digital architects do not think of the "performative inhabitant" as a passive user or a simple receptor of architecture. On the contrary, the inhabitant is imagined by digital architects is as an active agent (and an activator) into architectural space.[37] In consequence, when architecture is constructed as a responsive

Figure 2.8

device, capable to address the various conditions and requirements of a given context, the users and the buildings are considered as constitutive parts of the same system. Thus, in performance-based architecture the perceptions and the actions of the inhabitants can be considered as inputs that inform the design process, or even as actuators that transform the built space. In this way, from the performative view, buildings are considered as *open systems*[38] that should not act as normative artifacts that frame the way of life of a typified user, but as interfaces,[39] as mediation artifacts that should permit the emergence of different use conditions – think, for instance, of Cedric Price's Fun Palace, a paradigmatic architectural project that has influenced a whole generation of digital architects.

As the performative inhabitant emerged as the user of cybernetic architecture, digital architects have found more accurate metaphors of the human body (as model of the building) in a series of concepts employed by contemporary thinkers to explain the contemporary human condition. Among these concepts are the hybrid, the nomad, the cyborg, and the parasite, which in digital design thinking replace the customary architectural references to the ideal human body, which have been present in western architectural discourse from classical times to modernity.[40]

The abovementioned references to new constructions of the human body reveal how, beyond the technical aspects of computer-based design, the leading models of digital architecture have drawn from diverse ideas and concepts inherited from a variety of contemporary scientific fields and theories. More importantly, as will be seen in the next chapters, the different constructions of digital architecture informed by these scientific fields and theories have returned recursively to the main themes fostered by the discourses of performance discussed previously: the conception of buildings as dynamic systems, as devices highly integrated with the environment, as communicational and sentient artifacts ruled by flows of information.

The above is the reason why I consider the concept of performance as the key notion to comprehend the evolution of digital architecture. It is also the reason to analyze the productions of digital architects not only in terms of the impact in the profession of the pragmatics of the computer, but in relation to the influence of the informational ontology embodied by the discourses of performance-based architecture. This is the central question addressed by the following chapters, in which I attempt to present a comprehensive account of the evolution of the computational perspective in architecture from the perspective of the spread of cybernetic ideas into diverse fields of knowledge that, as a result of the triangulation effect discussed by Bowker,[41] have shaped the imagination of digital architecture. To do this, I will explore to what extent the performative/cybernetic conceptions of design issues discussed above are at the core of the dominant constructions in this field, which I classify according to three main categories: architectural systems, genetic mechanisms, and complex phenomena.

At this point it is necessary to clarify that the decision to classify the productions of digital architecture according to well defined categories is, in a certain way, arbitrary. Digital architecture is a highly interdisciplinary field that draws from several crossed references to many techno-scientific fields. For this reason, numerous explorations of digital design could be situated simultaneously in more than one of the proposed categories (or other categories that this survey does not consider). Thus, the decision to establish a direct connection among a certain type of architectural approach and a particular framework of reference is somewhat reductive. To justify this simplification, the anthropologist Gregory Bateson (a cybernetitian!) offers a reasonable explanation of the need to use categories to analyze cultural productions. For Bateson, categories are not real subdivisions, they are abstractions that we create for convenience reasons to facilitate the task of describing an object of study.[42] In what regards my analysis of the cybernetic constructions of digital architecture, the choice of grouping different architectural practices under a common category, and to analyze them according to their most obvious connections to a specific model of thought, aims to highlight the centrality of the informational paradigm in such practices. More precisely, the proposed classification allows me to trace the relationship among the cybernetic imagination of architecture, the elaboration of new frameworks for architectural practice informed by fields connected to the cybernetic framework (systems thinking, molecular biology and bioinformatics, as well as complexity theory), and the different scenarios of computer-mediated design that have emerged hand in hand with these constructions of the disciplinary problems. Having said the above, it should be remembered, with Bateson, that cultural productions are not the labels that we use for the analysis.

Notes

1 See in this respect: Michael Hensel, *Performance-Oriented Architecture: Rethinking Architectural Design and the Built Environment.*
2 Ibid.
3 Ibid.
4 Crucially, according to Hensel's history of the notion of performance, there is a clear connection between the emergence of notions such as *environment*, *milieu,* and *Umwelt* and the rise in the early twentieth century of systems thinking. As we will see, systemic thinking coincided with the cybernetic model in its conception of the world according to a relational logic.
5 Aaron Sprecher, "Informationism: information as architectural performance," 27.
6 Kalay, "Performance-based design," 400.
7 For a broad survey of the evolution of the discourses of performance in architecture, see: Kolarevic & Malkawi, *Performative Architecture;* Neuman & Grobman, *Performalism*; Grobman, "The various dimensions of the concept of performance;" Hensel, *Performance-oriented architecture.*
8 Moe & Smith, "Introduction. Systems, technics and society."
9 Kiesler, "On correalism and biotechnique."
10 See: Picon, *Digital Culture in Architecture.* See also: Picon, "Architecture as performative art."
11 Progressive Architecture, "Performance Design."
12 The central question of *The Sciences of the Artificial* was to describe an intellectual structure to accommodate the empirical phenomena that are artificial, as opposed to natural phenomena. This question reveals the close connection of Herbert's ideas and the cybernetic paradigm. As a matter of fact, Simon defines as "artificial" those systems that have a specific form or behavior that is a response to the conditions of a given environment. Accordingly, for Simon, the conditions of existence of an artificial system are not defined by its internal organization but as the result of a negotiation with the outer environment.
13 Simon, *The sciences of the artificial*, 116.

14 Progressive Architecture, "Performance Design."
15 According to Geof Bowker's analysis of the rhetoric strategies employed by the cyberneticians to legitimize the informational approach, the move of the promoters of the model, aimed at signaling the link between *Performance Design* and the "cybernetic revolution," can be read as an attempt to gain recognition by claiming the connection of the proposed design approach to a framework that by the late 1960's had reached a prominent place in scientific circles.
16 In the mentioned article, Hight reminds the need of formulating architectural questions in connection to the problems studied by architecture. Interestingly, he does so by means of a cybernetic construction of design issues.
17 Hight, "High-performance anxiety," 41–42.
18 Ibid, 41.
19 Ibid, 42.
20 Spuybroek, "The Structure of Vagueness," 167.
21 Lynn, *Animate Form,* 11.
22 Van Berkel & Bos, "Diagrams."
23 Zaera Polo, "Between Ideas and Matters."
24 This design research is particularly relevant in the history of the evolution of digital design methods. Alexander does not only address a paradigmatic conception of architecture based on the idea that a series of contextual forces can produce a given architectural form. He also implies that, from this perspective, time is a relevant constraint of design practice because to make a good it is necessary to process great amounts of data. This question is central to several digital design practices that since the 1960´s have constructed design as a computational problem.
25 Alexander, *Notes on the Synthesis of Form*, 3.
26 Ibid., 15–16.
27 Rahim, *Catalytic Formations.*
28 Oxman, "Theory and design in the first digital age."
29 The work of a pre-digital architect like Frederick Kiesler is representative of how, as new conceptions of the built environment emerged, architects started to imagine new formal vocabularies that express such ideas. Kiesler, who wrote the seminal article *On Correalism and Biotechnique* (which describes an early systems approach to architectural problems), also explored ideas about spatial continuity in the project "Endless Space" (which challenged the Euclidian representation of space). This project was part of the 1960 exhibition *Visionary Architecture,* held at the Museum of Modern Art in New York, which displayed a series of projects that, back then, were considered too revolutionary to be built.
30 Oxman, "Theory and design in the first digital age," 252.
31 In this respect, it is interesting to recall Jean-François Lyotard's thesis about the connection between the emergence of the informational paradigm and what he calls the post-modern condition; see: Lyotard, *The Postmodern Condition.* This idea offers some clues to grasp the relevance of digital culture in the explorations of digital architects.
32 Think, for instance, of the famous study houses by Peter Eisenman, one of the key promoters of information-driven design methods.
33 Lafontaine, *L'empire cybernétique.*
34 Breton, *L'utopie de la communication.*
35 Ibid.
36 See in this respect: Bateson, *Steps to an ecology of mind.*
37 At this point appears, once again, the paradigm shift inherent to the *performative turn.* From the perspective of the performance paradigm, human acts are considered as performed actions. This idea implies the conception of the subject as an active agent.

38 See in this respect my discussion, in chapter 3, of the influence of the key ideas of systems thinking in digital architecture.
39 See in this respect: Diller and Scoffidio, "Corps, l'espace prescrit."
40 For a comprehensive analysis of this subject, see: Hight, *Architectural principles in the age of cybernetics*. In this book, the author examines how the conception of the body as a central concept of architectural discourse has changed during the last decades, within a cultural and technological context that corresponds to the period of development of information technologies and informational thinking.
41 Bowker, "How to be universal."
42 Bateson, "Steps to an ecology of mind. "

Bibliography

Alexander, Christopher. *Notes on the Synthesis of Form*. Cambridge, MA: Harvard University Press, 1973.

Bateson, Gregory. *Steps to an Ecology of Mind: Collected Essays in Anthropology, Psychiatry, Evolution, and Epistemology*. Chigago: University of Chicago Press, 2000.

Bowker, Geof. "How to Be Universal: Some Cybernetic Strategies, 1943–70." *Social Studies of Science* 23, no. 1 (1993).

Breton, Philippe. *L'utopie de la Communication: Le Mythe du Village Planetaire*. Paris: La decouverte, 1995.

Diller, Elizabeth, and Ricardo Scoffidio. "Corps, l'espace Prescrit." *Techniques et Architecture* 429 (1997).

Grobman, Yasha J. "The Various Dimensions of the Concept of Performance in Architecture." In *Performalism. Form and Performance in Digital Architecture*. Edited by Eran Neuman and Yasha J. Grobman, 9–13. London, New York: Routledge, 2012.

Hensel, Michael. *Performance-Oriented Architecture: Rethinking Architectural Design and the Built Environment*. John Wiley & Sons, 2013.

Hight, Christopher. "High-Performance Anxiety." In *Performalism. Form and Performance in Digital Architecture*. Edited by Eran Neuman and Yasha J Grobman, 37–42. London, New York: Routledge, 2012.

—. *Architectural Principles in the Age of Cybernetics*. New York: Routledge, 2008.

Kalay, Yehuda E.. "Performance-Based Design." *Automation in Construction* 8 (1999): 395–409.

Kiesler, Frederick. "On Correalism and Biotechnique: a Definition and Test of a New Approach to Building Design." *Architectural Record* 86, no. 3 (1939): 60–75.

Kolarevic, Branko, Ali M Malkawi. *Performative Architecture. Beyond Instrumentality*. Edited by Branko Kolarevic and Ali M Malkawi. New York, London: Spon Press, 2005.

Lafontaine, Céline. *L'empire Cybernétique. Des Machines à Penser à La Pensée Machine*. Paris: Editions du Seuil, 2004.

Lynn, Greg. *Animate Form*. New York: Princeton Architectural Press, 1999.

Lyotard, Jean François. *The Postmodern Condition: A Report on Knowledge*. Minneapolis: University of Minnesota Press, 1984.

Moe, Kiel, Ryan E Smith. "Introduction. Systems, Technics and Society." In *Building Systems: Design Technology and Society*. Edited by Kiel Moe and Ryan E Smith, 1–10. New York: Routledge, 2012.

Oxman, Rivka. "Theory and Design in the First Digital Age." *Design Studies* 27 (2006): 229–65.

Picon, Antoine. "Architecture as Performative Art." In *Performalism. Form and Performance in Digital Architecture*. Edited by Neuman Eran and Yasha J Grobman, 15–19. London – New York: Routledge, 2012.

—. *Digital Culture in Architecture. An Introduction for the Design Professions*. Basel: Birkhauser GMBH, 2010.

Progresive Architecture. "Performance Design." *Progresive Architecture* (1967): 104–153.

Rahim, Ali. *Catalytic Formations. Architecture and Digital Design*. Oxon: Taylor & Francis, 2006.

Simon, Herbert A. *The Sciences of the Artificial*. Cambridge, MA/London: The MIT Press, 1996.

Sprecher, Aaron. "Informationism: Information as Architectural Performance." In *Performalism. Form and Performance in Digital Architecture* Edited by Neuman Eran and Yasha J Grobman, 27–31. London, New York: Routledge, 2012.

Spuybroek, lars. "The Structure of Vagueness." In *Performative Architecture. Beyond Instrumentality*. Edited by Branko Kolarevic and Ali M. Malkawi, 161–176. New York: Spoon Press, 2005.

Van Berkel, Ben, and Caroline Bos. "Diagrams." In *The Diagrams of Architcture*. Edited by Mark Garcia, 222–227. London: Wiley, 2010.

Zaera Polo, Alejandro. "Between Ideas and Matters. Icons, Indexes, Diagrams, Drawings and Graphs." In *The Diagrams of Architecture*. Edited by Mark Garcia, 237–244. London: Wiley, 2010.

3 Architectural systems

In his book, *Architectures of Time*, the architectural theorist Sanford Kwinter discusses the transformation of twentieth-century epistemology, and he explains how the world of physics gave way to the world of biology as a model of both scientific and metaphysical explanation. According to Kwinter, such transformation would explain the paradigm shift in architectural thinking discussed in Chapter 2; it is a change in the way we think of the disciplinary issues which is represented by the departure in contemporary architectural practices from the conception of building as individual and static objects. In opposition to the static conception of architectural objects, in contemporary architectural thinking, particularly in the world of digital architecture, it has been common to think of buildings and the urban space as the set of relations among diverse elements that compose a system. For Kwinter, the former implies that "the object – be it a building, a compound site, or an entire urban matrix, insofar as such unities continue to exist at all as functional terms – would be defined now not by how it appears, but rather by practices: those it partakes of and those that take place within it."[1] The author argues that according to this re-conception of the built environment "the unitariness of the object would necessarily vanish – deflected now into a single but double articulated field (relations, by definition, never correspond to objects.)."[2] In addition, he claims that from this perspective, the built space is now characterized by the relationships that are smaller than the objects as well as the relations or systems that contain them. He refers to these relations as "micro-architectures" and "macro-architectures," a definition of the built environment that is essentially a translation into architectural language of the conception of things fostered by systems thinking; that is, the definition of diverse phenomena as systems, as forms of organization composed of various interrelated elements, or sub-systems, and as components into larger meta-systems that contain them.

As discussed in Chapter 2, the abovementioned conception of architecture gained momentum in the second part of the twentieth century, and it was central to the work of the architects and design theorist who, at the dawn of digital architecture, started to explore possible applications

DOI: 10.4324/9781003181101-3

of information technology in architectural practice. In addition, we have seen that the early explorations of computer-based design adopted the central concepts of Systems Analysis, a framework that described engineering design as the search of the proper fit among a set of alternatives of action (the command variables) and a set of conditions defined by the context of development of a given design problem (environmental parameters).[3] Ever since, this kind of analysis of design problems has been at the core of the work of digital architects, who have explored in broader terms a systemic conception of architecture and design.[4] Crucially, such explorations have fostered the cybernetic imagination of architecture by means of the construction of architectural problems in reference to the main ideas advanced by systems thinkers such as Ervin Laszlo and Ludwig von Bertalanffy, whose *General Systems Theory* shared several aspects with the cybernetic paradigm.

In the following pages, I will discuss the key ideas advanced by systems thinkers, their links with the cybernetic framework, and I their influence on some paradigmatic constructions of architectural issues promoted by digital architects. Through this survey, I will also trace the connection between the systems view of architecture and the prevalent use of biological narratives in digital architecture. This analysis permits me to claim that the cybernetic description of natural phenomena as open systems, which underlies to the main ideas endorsed by systems thinking, explains the widespread trend in digital architecture to rely on organic accounts of design and to investigate the formation of architecture as a processes inspired by biological notions. Following Kwinter's claim regarding the rise of the world of biology as a model of both scientific and metaphysical explanation, I will trace the connection between the emergence of biology as a model of explanation in digital architecture and the expansion in western knowledge of cybernetic idioms. As discussed previously, the spread of cybernetic narratives contributed to blur the separation between the natural and the artificial in contemporary scientific models. Crucially, in systems thinking such separation disappeared with the conceptualization of biological phenomena as information-based systems, an idea that was later extrapolated to the explanation of phenomena of another nature.

General systems theory

As mentioned earlier, in Chapter 2, it was discussed that one of the central aspects of the performative imagination of architecture was the construction of the profession as a subsidiary practice of Systems Analysis. Ever since, the holistic conception of things has been at the core of the explorations of digital architecture, in which buildings have been frequently imagined as the result of the complex interaction among the various factors that define a spatial reality, as self-regulated mechanisms that achieve a state of equilibrium with their environment, and as systems that mimic the functioning of natural phenomena. As we will see, these views of architectural issues are directly connected to the central themes of Systems Theory, as exposed in the influential works of the Austrian biologist Ludwig von Bertalanffy and other systems thinkers.

Probably, the most important idea of von Bertalanffy's theory is the description of organisms as open systems, exposed in the author's influential book *General Systems Theory*. It is a conception of natural phenomena which is grounded on an informational explanation of living beings and that shares several aspects with the cybernetic conception of things. In accordance with some ideas broadly discussed in academic circles during the second half of the twentieth century, von Bertalanffy imagined a formulation of the organism as a sort of self-regulated form of organization. According to the systems view, the organism is a feedback system able to keep a state of equilibrium thanks to its interactions with the surrounding environment.

Von Bertalanffy saw his description of the organism as a critique of the mechanist conception of modern science; that is, the scientific method described by Descartes' second rule, consisting in fragmenting a problem of study in simple and separate elements. According to this mechanist approach, the scientific practice is about reducing complex phenomena to their elemental parts and processes and then to reunite them either conceptually or experimentally in order to objectify the studied phenomenon. This is the same approach fostered by the classical Newtonian methodology, which was grounded on the construction of the object of study as a set of isolated elements, from which it was intended to deduce general properties without taking into account the relationship between the parts that constitute the studied phenomenon.[5] For von Bertalanffy, in biological sciences, this kind of approach denied the essential aspect of the phenomenon of life. In opposition to the reductionist paradigm, the systems view promoted an organic conception of biological sciences that made evident the importance of considering the organism as an organized whole, and it aimed at discovering organization principles at all levels.[6] Therefore, for von Bertalanffy, the study of biologic phenomena should not be focused on the examination of their parts independently, but on the relations among them. According to this idea, he defined systems as a set of interacting elements p that are linked by relations R, where the behavior of p changes depending of the type of relation; therefore the behavior if p in R differs from the behavior of p in R'.[7] In other words, the systems view considers the interaction among the parts of a given organization as the key element for understanding its functioning. From this perspective, the comprehension of the relationships between the parts of a given system is more important than the comprehension of the individual action of its parts in isolation. This is the central idea represented by the systems thinking maxim that claims that a system is more than the sum of its parts.

The conception of things as open systems, initially imagined for the study of organisms, led von Bertalanffy and other scientists to study a variety of phenomena in diverse fields of knowledge as organized totalities. As a matter of fact, von Bertalanffy imagined *General Systems Theory* as a model to study from the same perspective a variety of problems in divergent fields which included, in addition to biology, behavioral science, and sociology. His proposal was to spread the informational conception of natural systems to other research problems by means of studying the structural similarity, or isomorphism, among them. This move implied to consider from the same perspective a variety of natural, physical and social phenomena, and to think about them in terms of three central concepts that structure the systems view of things: organization, totality, and teleology.

Organization, totality, and teleology

The notion of organization is the key concept of systems thinking. According to the systems view, living beings are organized phenomena, and this is the central element of the explanation of organisms as open systems. As mentioned before, the concept of open system describes organisms as forms of organization immersed in a permanent process of circular exchange with the environment. In other words, systems thinking considers organisms as feedback systems, that is, as negative entropy structures that evolve towards more elevated forms of organization. In this sense, in systems theory the notion of organization refers to the mechanisms that allow a system to reach a state of equilibrium, or even to reach more complex levels of organization, by means of its interaction with its surrounding environment.

The definition of systems, as forms of organization that result from the connection between a given system and a given environment, is inseparable from the conception of organized phenomena as totalities and as teleological phenomena. As a matter of fact, the consideration of organized phenomena as assemblages of interacting elements, as integrated wholes that seek equilibrium, is intrinsic to the concept of system. This idea is inherent to the holistic approach of the "relationality in the context" described by the systems approach. It is a way of thinking about things in the world that implies that the subtraction of an object of study from its context is an error derived from the linear explanations of causality.[8] In contrast with the linear explanations of modern science, and in accordance with the cybernetic logic of causality, systems thinking fosters the study of phenomena as a network of interrelated factors, as totalities that cannot be apprehended through the study of their parts as independent factors.

The holistic conception of things was central to the study of biological phenomena such as homeostasis and self-organization, which were of particular interest for systems thinkers. In consequence, the study of the self-regulating mechanisms observed in living systems implied to consider notions of teleology and directivity as valid research interests of systems thinking. Thus, in Systems Theory, the study of the teleological behavior of systems is not situated outside the limits of natural sciences, and the teleological explanation of the functioning of systems is not considered an anthropomorphic interpretation of the object of study. On the contrary, according to the systems framework, the teleological behavior of systems is considered a phenomenon that can be described in scientific terms and whose conditions and mechanisms need to be explained.[9]

As mentioned earlier, von Bertalanffy was convinced that these ideas could be employed for the explanation of a variety of phenomena in different research fields. In this respect, he sustained that diverse problems and similar concepts were developed in distinct fields of knowledge that differ substantially, and that the parallelism between those concepts highlighted the need to extend the conceptual schemes of systems thinking.[10] Accordingly, in his theory, he suggested the existence of models, principles, and laws that might be used in the study of a variety of systems independently of their nature. The above allowed the systems thinker to claim the legitimacy of his proposal of a general theory of systems, whose aim was to formulate universal principles for a variety of phenomena of scientific interest that could be described in similar terms.

The isomorphism and the unity of science

Under the premise that several phenomena could be explained as organized complexes, von Bertalanffy considered that the systems approach was a framework transferable to diverse disciplines. Even more, he conceived the idea of founding an inter-disciplinary theory based on a unitary conception of the world and the isomorphisms existing between various phenomena and fields of knowledge. In this way, the systems view appeared as a means to improve the exchange among different areas and to reduce the unnecessary multiplication of scientific models. In this sense, von Bertalanffy's project was to foster a "perspectivist" conception of science which (in opposition to the reductionist approach of modern science) aimed at finding laws inherent to the research objects of biology, sociology, and behavioral science. This was exactly what von Bertalanffy did with the aid of his colleagues of the *Society for General Systems Research,* who shared with him the belief that the systems view could be employed as a framework to analyze from the same perspective different problems in distinct fields of knowledge – the *Society for General Systems Research* gathered prominent researchers, such as the economist Kenneth E. Boulding, the bio-mathematician Anatol Rapaport and the physiologist Ralph Gerard, at the *Center for Advanced Study in the Behavioral Sciences* at Stanford University. Following the premises of *General Systems Theory,* the members of the *Society for General Systems Research* endorsed the systems view of the world and they fostered it by means of the study of two questions central to von Bertalanffy's project: the isomorphism between different research problems and the unity of science.

The fellows of the *Society for General Systems Research* believed that there were principles and scientific laws that could be applied to diverse research problems due to their structural similitude. For them, if two distinct research objects could be explained as the set of interrelated elements that produce a given form of organization, these different phenomena could be analyzed according to the same framework. More importantly, the isomorphism among diverse phenomena allowed them to imagine a unitary conception of the world. It was thanks to such unitary conception of things that they considered that the exchange among various fields of knowledge would reduce the unnecessary proliferation of scientific models. In consequence, they also considered that it was possible to establish a general theory able to describe valid principles for a variety of phenomena. Of course, such theory was Systems Theory, which provided a model of explanation of things grounded on the idea that several phenomena in the world could be explained as organized-teleological-holistic structures. In fact, this idea was at the core of von Bertalanffy's theory, which in his words, aimed at the search for general principles of systems, independently of their (biological, physical, or sociological) nature.[11]

Today there is no doubt that the pretentions of inter-disciplinarity and universality of systems thinking were amply satisfied. The systems view was not only adopted to analyze a variety of research problems in various fields of knowledge, but it raised to a world view from which the universe as a whole has been imagined as a complex meta-system composed by several entangled systems and sub-systems.

The systems view of the world

Thanks to the success of the systems approach, during the second half of the last century this framework became a preferred model to explain a variety of research objects in diverse fields that include economy, ecology, computer science, psychology, engineering, and architecture, of course. More importantly, the spread of systems thinking was a crucial factor that favored the expansion of the cybernetic view of the world as a complex apparatus constituted by dynamic, self-regulated, and interconnected systems. In this respect, the French philosopher Edgar Morin attributes to Systems Theory the emergence of a complex understanding of the world as a tissue of heterogeneous and inseparable elements.[12] More precisely, Morin considers the model inaugurated by von Bertalanffy the precursor of two ideas broadly accepted in contemporary thinking: on the one hand, the conception of the organization of systems as a problem of compensated disequilibrium and, on the other, the opinion that the intelligibility of a system should be sought in its relationship with the environment. According to Morin, these two ideas are on the basis of the mutation of the ontological status of the object – a mutation which is the product of considering various phenomena as self-organized systems and as phenomenally individual entities. According to the systems view, all things, even apparently autonomous entities, are in close contact with a given environment, and, in consequence, they are inseparable from it. From this perspective, in contemporary thinking objects are commonly considered as the product of a total adjustment among the phenomenal form (the context) and their internal organization principles.

The abovementioned ontological shift of the status of the object underlays the search of new models of knowledge where subject and object are integrated. Morin Claims that, in an epistemic sense, the systemic vision of things offered the answer to this search by showing that the object must be conceived as a part of an ecosystem and, more broadly, as a part of an open world and of a meta-system. According to this epistemology, the environment is part of the object and the object is part of the environment. Thus, for Morin, reality is now both in the connection and the distinction between a system and its environment, and the limit between them is always in an intermediary place among one and other; the limit is in the equilibrium achieved between the system and the environment, which is the condition of existence of both.[13]

The same view of things is expressed by the philosopher Ervin Laszlo, whose systemic philosophy is grounded on the concept of "natural system." Laszlo defines as natural systems all the structures that do not owe their existence to a conscious planning and which display any form of organization that is not the product of agents external to the system. For the author of *The Systems View of the World*, systems can be infra-organic, organic, or supra-organic, that is, physical, biological, and social, and they share four universally valid organizational constants present in any kind of system.[14]

First of all, says Laszlo, natural systems are totalities that display irreducible properties. For this reason, the study of systems must take into account the problem of organization and cannot be limited to the study of the parts of the system in isolation. The functioning of systems is based on the interaction among the components of the system, and such interaction can be comprised as a communicational process, regardless of whether these interactions take place among a group of atoms or among the individuals in a social group.[15] Such communicational character guarantees the second organizational constant of natural systems; namely, their capacity to self-regulate their behavior in a dynamic environment. Since systems are not static, they have a tendency to develop, evolve, and degrade. So, from the atom to the most complex social organization, systems present mechanisms of adjustment, adaptation, and preservation of a state of equilibrium. In addition to the capacity to self-regulate, systems are self-creating mechanisms that form themselves as a reaction to the stimulus they receive from the environment.[16] The third constant is that all systems are open to the influence of the external world and react to it; in this way, they are implicated in a permanent exchange process where each system affects its surrounding environment and vice versa.[17] From the above it follows that the world is a sort of complex meta-system constituted by a hierarchy of sub-systems that go across the regions of the physical, the biological and the social. In this sense, although systems can be clearly differentiated, they can be part of other arrangements; this is the fourth constant of systems.[18] According to the fourth condition, systems are always interfaces, that is, they are components that coordinate the relationship among diverse parts and functions; humans, for instance, are integrated wholes in biological terms, but in sociological terms they are components of the social system.

The organizational constants of systems described by Laszlo reveal the close relationship between the systems view of the world and the informational ontology fostered by cybernetics. Laszlo's description of the organizational constants of systems is based on four key aspects that systems thinking shares with the cybernetic model. First, the description of the functioning of things as a communicational process; second, the conception of systems as self-regulated devices; third, the description of self-regulation as a process that involves the exchange of information with an outer environment; and finally, the idea that the universe as a whole can be conceived as a sort of negative feedback system.

The cybernetics of the systems view

The above are not the only aspects that the systems view shares with the cybernetic framework. Among other aspects shared by cybernetics and systems thinking can be mentioned the holistic vision of things fostered by the two models, the critique of the linear and reductionist conception of modern science inherent to their explanations of the nature of things, the use of a common language to describe their research problems, and, of course, the ambitions of universality claimed by both frameworks.

As a matter of fact, several scholars have pointed out the correspondence among systems thinking and cybernetics. François Dosse, for instance, claims that the systems view can be understood as an extension of structuralism. According to Dosse, structuralism and systems theory share the same ideals of scientism and universality, the holistic conception of the world and a penchant towards interdisciplinarity. In addition, he claims that cybernetics constitutes the link among the two models by pointing that the cybernetic framework played a key role in the development of both fields.[19] Edgar Morin shares the opinion of Dosse, and he adds that systems thinking and cybernetics share the same "fruitful aspects"; namely, the use of the concept of machine as a means to describe organized systems.[20] In addition, Céline Lafontaine suggests that the systems view makes part of the constellation of disciplines that revolve around biology, communication science and cognitive science. For the author of *L'empire Cybérnetique,* it is possible to claim that the influence of cybernetics was reinforced by systems thinking – particularly in what concerns the theories of self-organization, central to second-order cybernetics.[21] This connection appears clearly if one considers the work of the British cybernetitian William Ross Ashby and the later work of some of the most influential theorists of self-organization, such as Humberto Maturana and Francisco Varela.[22]

Actually, the coincidences between systems theory and cybernetics are so abundant that some authors consider both frameworks one and the same.[23] Indeed, von Bertalanffy was the first to recognize the close connections between cybernetics and systems theory. For instance, in the introduction to *General Systems Theory*, he quotes a conference offered by the cybernetitian Lawrence K. Frank, where he argues in favor of the cybernetic methodologies for the study of self-regulated processes, of systems and of self-directed organisms.[24] Other authors cited by von Bertalanffy include William Ross Ashby, Stafford Beer, Heinz von Foerster, William Gray Walter, Lawrence S. Kubie, Warren McCulloch, John von Neumann, Claude Shannon, Warren Weaver, and Norbert Wiener; that is, the principal participants of the *Macy Conferences*. In addition, von Bertalanffy also quotes other prominent researchers indirectly connected to the raise of cybernetic thinking and computer science that include Walter B. Cannon and Alan Turing.

Furthermore, in von Bertalanffy's notes about the development of the mathematical theory of systems, he defines systems in the same terms employed by Wiener for the study of servomechanisms. For instance, in his description of the notion of system, von Bertalanffy uses the cybernetic metaphor of the black box, and the relationship among the system and the environment is described according to Claude Shannon's model of communication. More importantly, as mentioned earlier, the description of the central concept of the open system is based on the cybernetic model of circular causality. Even more, the description of the open system evokes a series of cybernetic notions that include the definition of systems as feedback mechanisms, as information-based forms of organization, and as negentropic phenomena.

Such characterizations of systems demonstrate to what extent the key concepts of systems thinking – totality, organization and integration – are closely connected to the central notions of cybernetic thinking – homeostasis, self-regulation, circular causality. The former also explains the cybernetic ascendancy of the organic conceptions of society (Parsons, Luhman), of economy (Hayek, Kelly), and of the world in general (Odum), that emerged under the systems view during the late twentieth century.[25] The same can be said about the mutation of the ontological status of the object referred by Morin, which underlays to the systemic conception of the built environment evoked by Kwinter in *Architectures of Time* – a conception that implied the departure in contemporary architectural discourse from the construction of buildings as individual and static objects. In the next

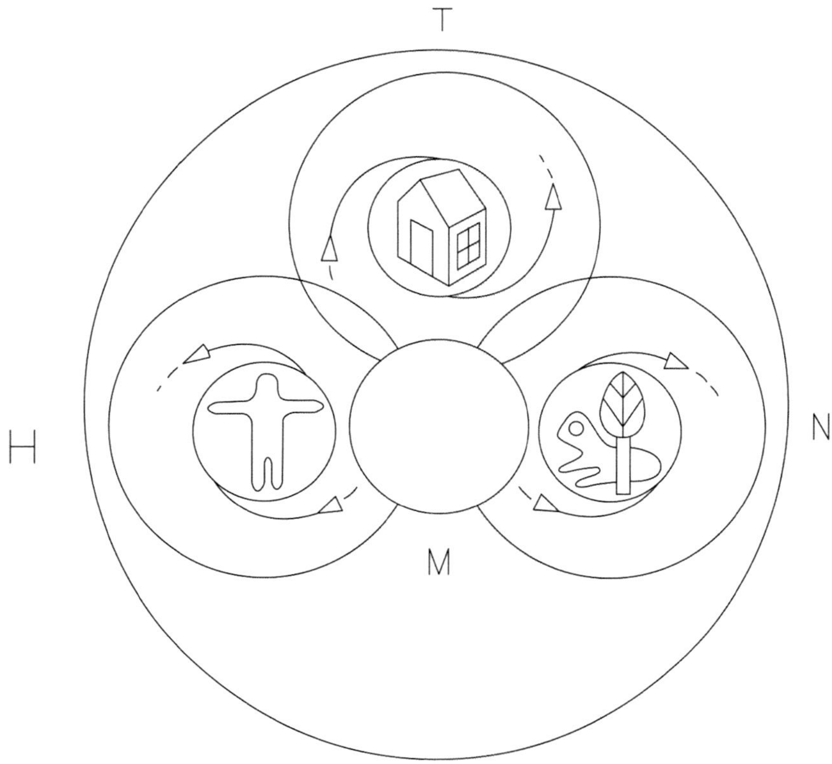

Figure 3.1

section, I will discuss to what extent the cybernetic/systemic conception of architectural issues can be traced in the constructions of digital architecture, and how this view of the disciplinary problems allowed the emergence of a biological paradigm in the explanations of digital architecture.

The systems view in architecture

Previously, I have argued that the holistic conception of the built environment is one of the key themes of digital architecture and that, in accordance with this vision of the disciplinary issues, the description of buildings as sorts of self-regulated, sentient and semi-organic devices has been a recursive question in computer-based architectural productions. In fact, such constructions of the disciplinary problems have been so broadly explored by digital architects that some prominent practitioners and theorists see in the systems view of architecture a sort of doctrine, movement, or mode of production which has directed the digital turn in the profession.

For instance, Yasha J. Neuman and Eran Gromban coined the term *performalism* to describe what they consider a new form of avant-garde architecture that would be at the core of the practice of several digital architects. For Neuman and Grobman, the performance approach, considered as an "ism," defines a tendency in contemporary architectural practices to construct design problems according to "similar ideas and forms of production."[26] Importantly, they argue that this trend does not define a new architectural style. On the contrary, they claim that *performalism* is a trend that embodies a change of paradigm in architectural thinking that resonates with the transformations described by Kwinter. For the editors of *Performalism*, such transformations define "the search for a new logic in the conception of form and a new relationship between different parties in the triangle Form-Function-Subject"[27] grounded on the idea that form is the result of performance. In this sense, the architectural object appears as the result of the combination of several (empiric, cognitive, perceptive) aspects that redefine the problems of form and function, object and subject, space and body, perception and cognition, politics and ideology in the contemporary production of space.[28]

Possibly, the best example of the trend described by Neuman and Gromban is Patrick Schumacher's *Parametricist Manifesto*, that could be defined as the architect's guide to systemic architecture. Indeed, Schumacher's theory of "parametricism" is based on a series of concepts exposed by systems thinkers such as Niklas Luhman, in the field of sociology, and Humberto Maturana and Francisco Varela, in the field of natural sciences.[29] In reference to the ideas about society and natural systems developed by these scholars, Schumacher advances a systemic definition of architecture presented in an article titled *Architecture's next ontological innovation*. Schumacher's definition of architecture is grounded on the principle that "the elements or primitives of architecture have become parametrically malleable and remain dynamically embedded in networks of dependency, including multiple aspects of the context; all subsystems are internally differentiated and are to be correlated with (all) the other subsystems."[30] In addition, Schumacher claims that "everything must resonate with everything else. This should result in an overall intensification of relations that gives the urban field a performative density, informational richness, and cognitive coherence that makes for quick navigation and effective participation in a complex social arena."[31] For Schumacher, the essential aspect of contemporary cultural advancement is our ability to "move through a rapid succession of communicative encounters."[32] To acquire this capacity we need a "new built environment with an unprecedented level of complexity, a complexity that is organized and articulated into a complex, variegated order of the kind we admire in natural, self-organized systems."[33]

Actually, Schumacher's next ontological innovation is not really new. Indeed, the ontology of the built environment advanced by Schumacher revisits the cybernetic descriptions of architecture embraced by digital architects since the beginnings of the computational perspective in the profession. However, it is interesting to note how in his discourse these descriptions are restated in terms of some of the main themes of systems thinking. In Schumacher's description of architecture buildings and the city are constructed as complex dynamic systems and forms of organization that should display the distinctive character of natural systems; namely, their ability to self-organize their development. In the same way, conceived as a system, the built space becomes an apparatus that should permanently exchange information, matter and energy with its context to reach higher levels of order.

The conception of architectural space as a system implies the definition of corresponding modes of production of space. Consequently, in digital architecture practices, the corollary of the systemic imagination of architecture is the development of alternative design methods based on the exploration of a relational logic in design. As it is explained by Kiel Moe and Ryan E. Smith, the systems approach in architecture implies the definition of the parts of the project, its connections and its networks of action. It is by means of this kind of epistemology of design that in many contemporary practices of architecture are defined aspects of function, scale, and scope that involve procedures based on notions of hierarchy, inputs and outputs, and degrees of dynamic equilibrium.[34] The above approach to the solution of architectural problems is at the core of the development of several computer-based design methods, in which design is usually redefined as a search space that involves the analysis of a series of interrelated actors, factors and forces that participate in the materialization of architecture. Let's see to what extent this conception of design rewrites the main concepts of systems thinking: organization, totality, and integration.

We have already seen that, from a systems perspective, the elements of architecture are dynamically embedded in networks of dependency that include multiple aspects of the context. In this sense, buildings are considered as organized totalities and as dynamic objects highly integrated with the environment. According to this conception of the built space, the

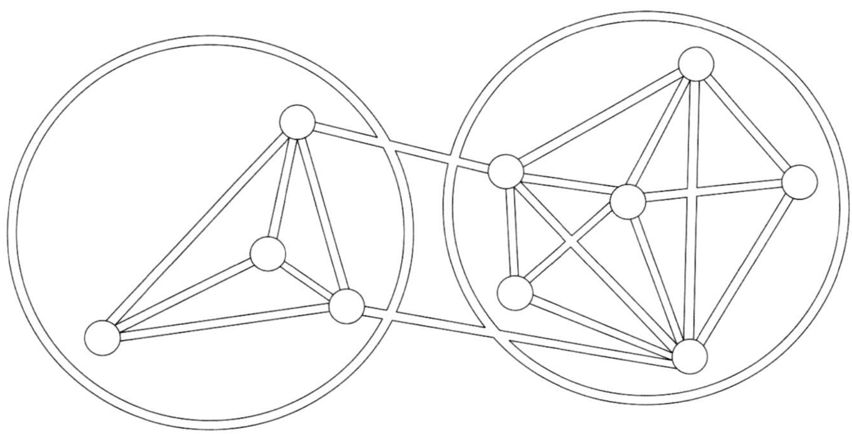

Figure 3.2

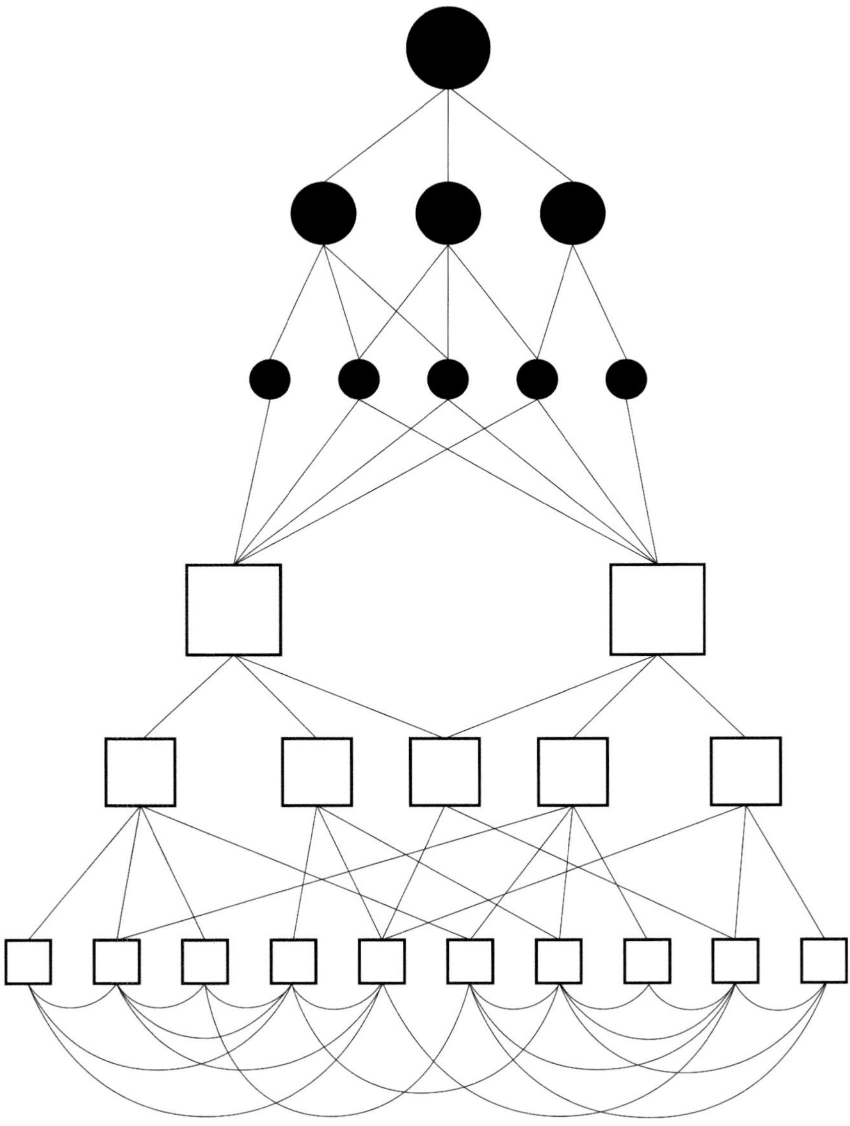

Figure 3.3

purpose of design is to find the proper equilibrium between the architectural object and the context (a distinction that from the systemic perspective tends to disappear). These are the visions of architectural issues that emerged with the ontological mutation of architectural space mentioned by Kwinter, which in the productions of digital architecture have challenged the static and individual character attributed to buildings traditionally. Accordingly, from a systems perspective, digital architects have endorsed

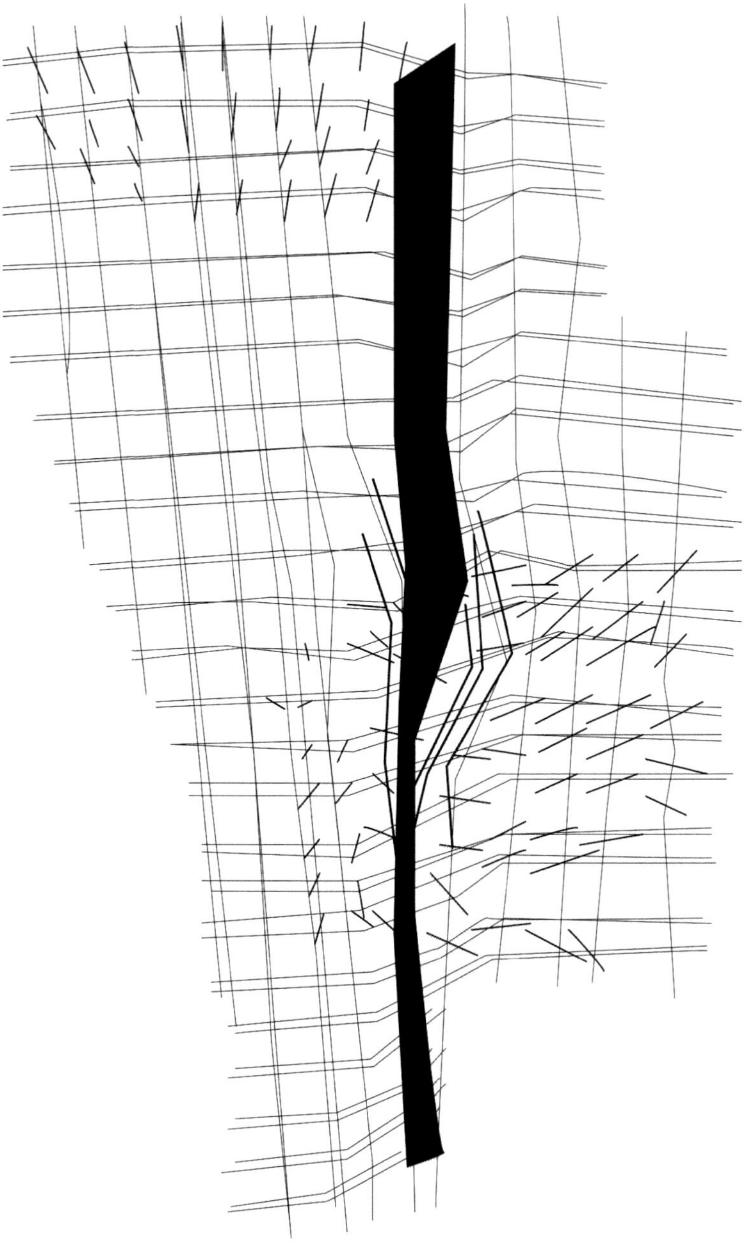

Figure 3.4

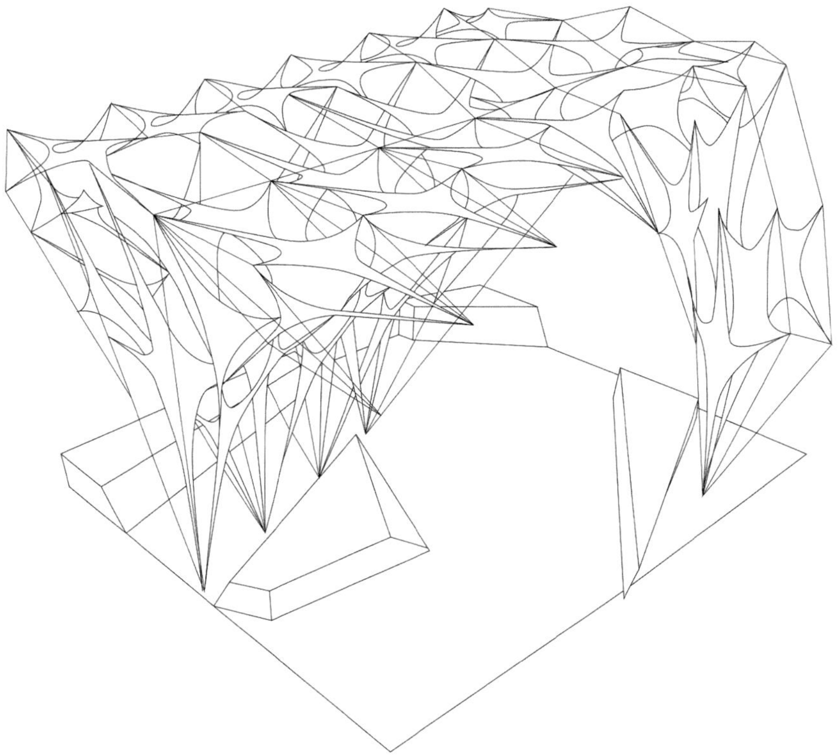

Figure 3.5

constructions of buildings as objects provided with agency, as mediation artifacts, as moments of a geometrical flux, as the embodiment of various interacting forces, and as self-regulating devices that must adjust their behavior to achieve a state of equilibrium.

As mentioned before, in systems thinking the notions of interaction and totality explain the existence of systems as arrangements that are the product of the coordinated action of discrete parts, as integrated wholes that cannot be apprehended by means of the individual analysis of the elements that compose them. Translated into architectural thinking, the holistic vision of things implies the construction of buildings (and design) as the product of complex dynamics that comprise material, constructive, social, and environmental factors. Take, for instance, Michael Hensel's systemic description of architecture. For Hensel, the built space is a "spatial material organization complex" that includes not only the material and spatial aspects of architecture, but also the subject and the environment. In this sense, Hensel claims that, according to the systemic construction of architectural problems, the conception of space shifts from the perception of the built environment as "a static organization that alone defines an object to intricate processes of interaction and the capacities and transformations that arise from these interactions."[35] From this perspective, the formal and functional aspects of architecture are indivisible; considered as a spatial material organization complex, the built space is the result of four domains of action, subject, environment, matter, and space, that feedback each other. This idea is at the core of the *multi-performative* and *morfpho-ecologic* design models developed by Hensel and Achim Menges during the late 2000s, conceived as a means to achieve a high level of integration among the constructive system, the material aspects and the environmental phenomena that configure architectural space. Consequently, these design approaches imply thinking of architecture as the product of varied and dynamic relations between the material systems that compose the building, the environmental conditions to which it responds, and the use and perception of the designed object by the inhabitants.[36]

William Braham summarizes clearly this kind of design approach when he claims that, from a systems perspective, the different building systems cease to be considered optimized artifacts designed to accomplish specific functions to be considered complex systems which affect, globally and simultaneously, the building and the inhabitants as a whole.[37] The same idea is at the core of the work of Ali Rahim, who has claimed that "a desire to study the behavior of matter in its full complexity brings with it an ordering of the world where material systems are understood to be similarly cross-affiliated and in constant state of flux. The analytical approach to design, which studies a site or a project only from the top down, misses the properties that emerge from complex interactions between parts, as in the modernist notion of the diagram as a building parti."[38]

Both Braham's and Rahim's holistic descriptions of architecture and design issues evoke a series of themes frequently discussed by digital architects. Such themes include descriptions of architectural systems as ecologies, as mediation artifacts, as the substrate and catalyst of relationships among several components, and as the result of intricate entities in permanent movement. Behind these descriptions of architecture is an idea that has made a long way in the field digital architecture; namely, the conception of the built environment as an emergent reality.[39] This idea is at the core of different discourses about the autonomy of architecture and the subsequent "biologization" of design, common to the work of many digital architects.

The autonomy of architecture

One of the main consequences of thinking of architecture as a system and, ultimately, as an emergent phenomenon, was the appearance of the idea that architectural objects can be independent from a series of pre-established values related to matters of style, technique, and ideology. In the words of David Leatherbarrow, "when the building is freed from technological and aesthetic intentionalities, we discover its lateral connections

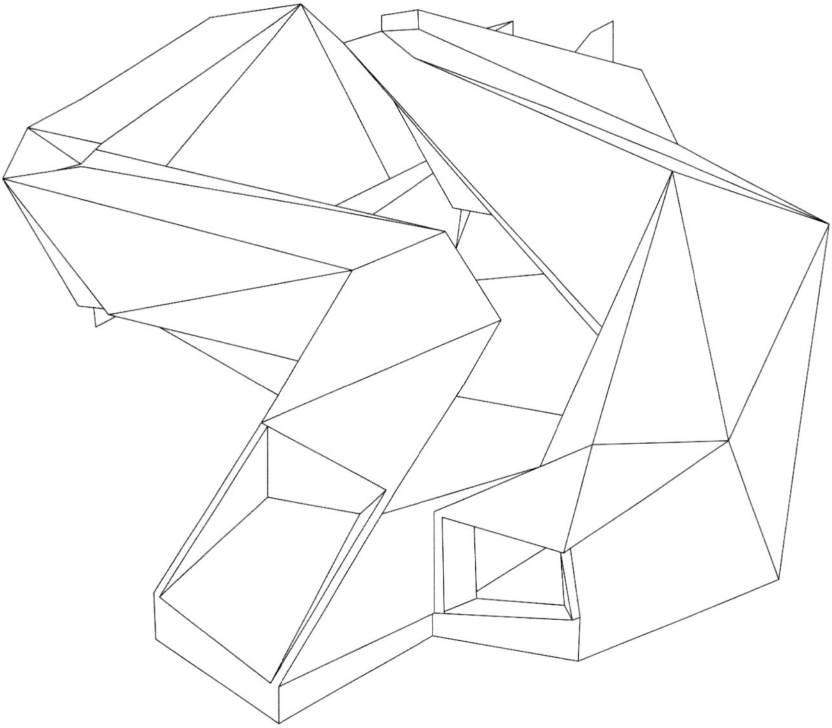

Figure 3.6

to an environmental and social milieu that is not of anyone's making, still less of design and planning...The point to be stressed is the buildings eccentricity, its existence outside of itself."[40]

Leatherbarrow's description of architectural space as an eccentric reality (that is, as something that exists outside itself) is representative of a question broadly discussed by digital architects. Namely, the construction of buildings as autonomous objects. It is a question that is inherent to the status assigned to buildings in digital architecture practices, but also to the epistemology of computer-based design. As explained by Leatherbarrow, this idea is directly connected to the construction of the architectural object as a spatial reality that emerges from "an environmental and social milieu." While this idea re-inscribes the systemic conception of architecture, it also questions the very notion of authorship in architectural design. If architectural space is the product of its lateral connections to a given context, then it follows, that the decisions made by the designer are somehow irrelevant. As a matter of fact, one of the key features of computational design methods is the partial or total automation of the design process. Interestingly, many digital architects have sought in the automation of design a means to solve the complex relations between the building and the context.

Figure 3.7

In digital architecture practices, the question of autonomy has been the corollary of the systems view, which, as we have seen, fostered a vision of the architectural object as a spatial reality that emerges from the complex relations among the elements that define a given design problem. Correspondingly, with the aid of computers, the act of design has been imagined as a matter of setting the rules for the automatic emergence of the building. In this way, the ontology of information and the pragmatics of information technology come together in different digital design approaches. Whereas the informational conception of things has allowed architects to think of architectural objects as emergent systems, the pragmatics of the computer has allowed them to think of design and, ultimately, the formation of buildings as a sort of self-directed and autonomous process – consider, for instance, Greg Lynn's concept of "delegation to the machine."

The above ideas underlie the work of several digital architects who, in accordance with them, have explored computer-based design scenarios that endorse the discourses about the autonomy of architecture in different degrees. They include the conception of the independence of the architectural object from any kind of determinism established by the designer, the imagination of the formation of architecture as an automated process, and an idea that is a corollary of the above, the construction of buildings as entities provided with agency. Of course, computational design tools have played a key role in this sense, since they allow architects to materialize in a design procedure the conception of the architectural object as something that can only be explained in terms of its behavior, independently from any established cannon. This kind of approach is central to the work of Lynn and other influential practitioners of digital design, whose projects and design processes embody a vision of the building as a system that takes shape within the dynamics of a material field and that is expressed as an effect. Take, for instance, the emblematic work of Peter Eissenman, which is a paradigmatic example of the conception of architecture conceived as an autonomous event. In this respect, Antoine Picon explains that, from this perspective, architecture becomes something that is only justified by what its presence produces and not by a set of values and images external to the performance of the building.[41]

It is interesting to notice the similitude between Picon's abovementioned description of buildings (as objects that are only justified by what their existence produce) and Kwinter's description of the ontological transformation of the architectural space, according to which buildings and the city are understood as systems that are defined not by their appearance but by the practices in which they are involved. Behind these descriptions of buildings is the third aspect connected to the visions about the autonomy of architecture that I mentioned before. I refer to the construction, in digital design practices, of buildings as entities provided with agency. This aspect offers a clue to understand the 'biologization' of design inherent to several explorations of digital architecture which, in turn, explain to what extent

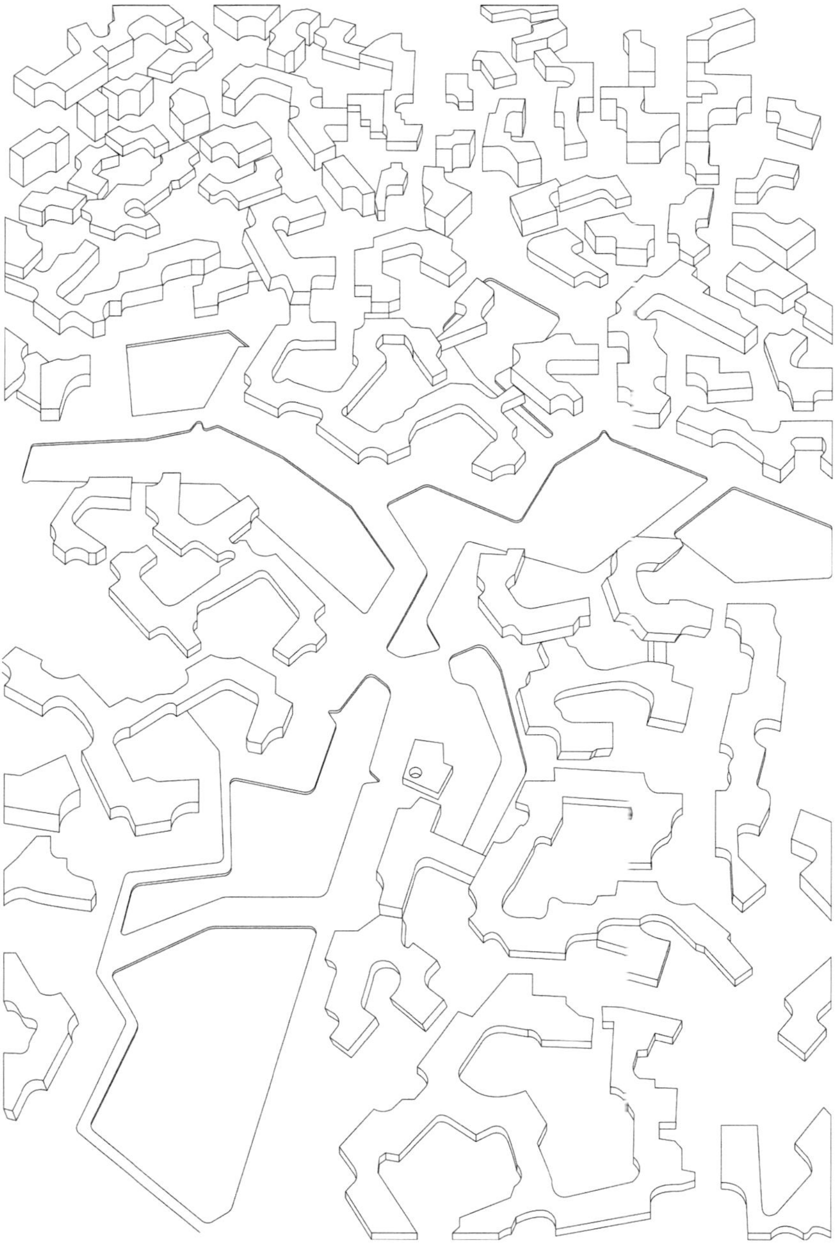

Figure 3.8

biology became a model of both scientific and metaphysical explanation in this field.

Biology as a model

Previously, I discussed to what extent the formal explorations of digital architecture are a search to accommodate the cybernetic conceptions of architectural space. In this regard, one may wonder how this search is connected to the proliferation of forms that evoke the world of nature in the productions of digital architects? A possible answer can be found in the way digital architects have constructed the problem of autonomy in relation to a series of concepts inherited from natural sciences. Think, for instance, of Schumacher's aforementioned claims about the autonomy of architecture, in which the concept of autonomy evokes a series of ideas borrowed from Humberto Maturana and Francisco Varela, champions of systems thinking in natural sciences.

Of course, Schumacher is not the only digital architect who has employed biological metaphors to explain the autonomous character attributed to architecture (as it is has been conceived under the systems view). As a matter of fact, several practitioners of digital design have fostered explanations of design issues grounded in biological concepts which promote the conception of architecture as a "natural system."[42]

Figure 3.9

Figure 3.10

Although the construction of architectural problems in reference to biological metaphors is not an exclusive feature of the work of digital architects (in fact, this kind of description has been a constant in the history of western architecture[43]), it is interesting to observe the great proliferation of organic narratives in this field. More importantly, it is interesting to see the connection among such organic narratives and the cybernetic imagination of design issues. For instance, the concept of homeostasis, which explains the process through which a living organism keeps a state of equilibrium, has been commonly employed by architects to characterize design problems as a matter of balance among various factors. Behind this biological construction of the architectural object are a series of ideas that recall the question of autonomy. Conceived as homeostatic phenomena, buildings appear as artifacts that result from changing environmental conditions, as forms of organization that adapt and evolve in response to such conditions, as systems that must achieve a balance relationship with the environment and, of course, as teleological systems that, like organisms, can do all this autonomously.

The same ideas lie beneath a variety of explorations of digital design which are grounded on descriptions of architecture as an adaptive and evolutionary mechanism, and as an emergent and self-organized system. Since the early days of digital architecture, the use of these biological concepts has been inherent to the elaboration of computer-based design methods, in which the production of form is imagined as a dynamic and self-directed system, and as the automated materialization of the variables, contained in a program, that define a spatial reality. Through the use of computer-based design techniques, and in reference to ideas and techniques imported from fields such as molecular biology, genetics and other branches of biology, many digital architects have fostered explanations of design as a generative process and of architecture as a programmed system. These conceptions of design have reinforced the informational imagination of architecture, in which designers are no longer seen as creators of forms, but as controllers of organic-like processes that define the conditions, interactions and parameters that shape architectural space. The outcome of such visions of design issues has been the replacement of traditional ideas about the production of space (as a closed, deterministic, and unidirectional act) by its conception as an open (adaptive and evolutionary) process. More recently, these ideas about design have been expressed in biological narratives in which buildings are described as emergent and self-organized systems – two notions that in contemporary natural sciences have been employed to describe organic phenomena whose organization is the product of the coordinated action of various elements without the mediation of a central control organ, such as the development of the body and the intelligent behavior.

Taking into account the above, it comes as no surprise that the spread of biological metaphors in the explanations of digital architecture has come hand in hand with the 'biologization' of architectural form. With the advent of computer-based design techniques, we have also witnessed the emergence of new formal vocabularies that replace traditional conceptions of space by a catalogue of forms that literally embody the techno-scientific references evoked by digital architects. While some of these explorations are symbolic representations of the concepts that inspire digital architects, other represent their attempts to take the biological imagination of design to a highly instrumental level, namely, to produce buildings that literally display the attributes of natural systems.

The proliferation of biological metaphors in the explanations of digital architecture reveal to what extent the world of biology has become a preferred model of explanation in this field. More precisely, this trend reveals how the expansion of cybernetic idioms – which, as we will see, is on the basis of the informational explanations of contemporary biology – underlies the biological turn in digital design thinking.

Crucially, various of the biological notions preferred by digital architects, including the abovementioned concepts (homeostasis, adaptation, evolution, emergence, heredity, and self-organization), are in the basis of the development of the cybernetic model, or were formulated (or reimagined) in contemporary natural sciences in reference to the cybernetic paradigm. For instance, the concept of homeostasis, coined by the French physiologist Claude Bernard, was a central reference in Wiener's description of self-regulated systems.[44] The notions of emergence and self-organization were central to the second wave of cybernetics and are the key concepts of complexity science, one of the most recent heirs of cybernetics thinking. And the concepts of adaptation and evolution were reimagined in contemporary biology according to the informational description of the mechanisms of heredity. Taking into account the above, Aaron Sprecher seems to

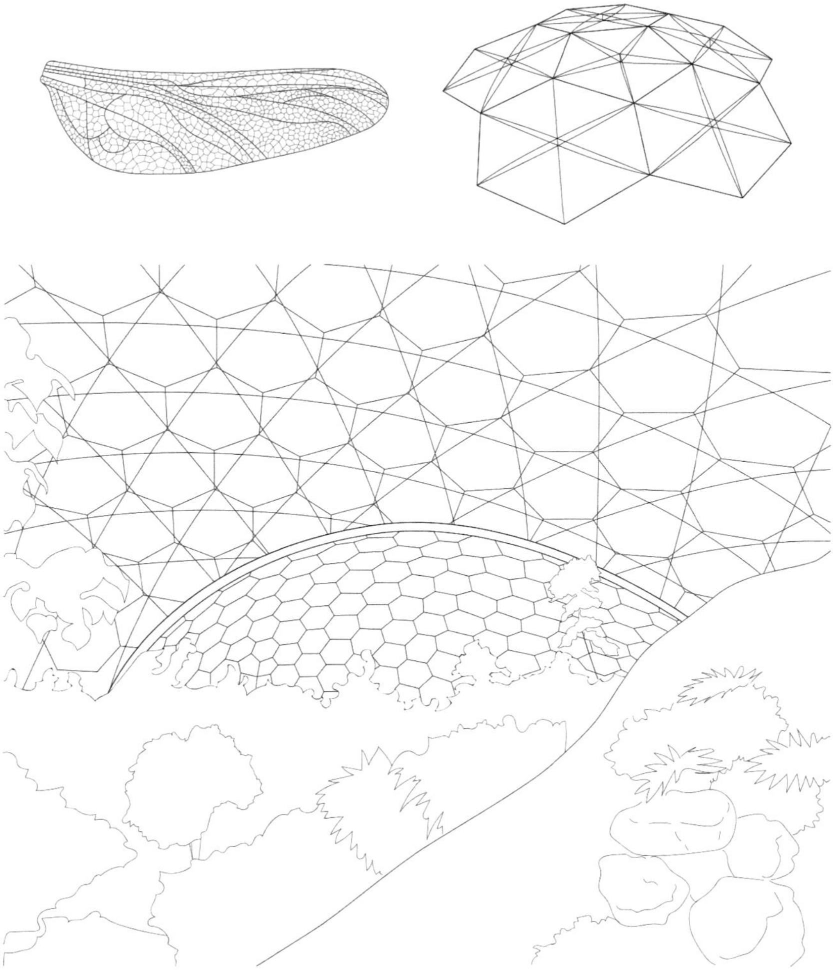

Figure 3.11

be right when he claims that it was the communicational conception of the nature of organisms and machines, as promoted by cybernetic thinking, what gave way to the new elaborations of architecture, in which buildings started to be imagined as natural systems. According to this conception of architectural issues the building "was no longer considered as a fixed entity but instead turned into a reactive system, a sort of semi-organic machine that could behave as a living organism."[45]

If cybernetitians are responsible for the rise of the communicational imagination of the nature of things, systems thinkers are largely responsible for the spread of this idea. In the same way that cyberneticians fostered the erasure of the limits between living and artificial phenomena, systems thinkers promoted the idea that several systems share the same organizational principles in spite of their biological, physical or sociological nature. Following this line of thought, the promoters of the systems view in architecture have fostered an imagination of design in which architectural objects are considered open systems; that is, self-regulated mechanisms and organized wholes. It is from this perspective that many digital architects have constructed design issues according to the logic of relational causality, and that they have imagined buildings as dynamic, interconnected, autonomous, and adaptive systems. As we have seen, the line that separates the conception of architectural objects as open systems and as sorts of semi-organic devices is extremely thin. The former explains why several digital architects have embraced biology as a valid explanation of design problems, either in metaphorical terms (through the use of biological narratives to explain the systemic nature of buildings), or through experimental approaches that aim to literally turn buildings into servomechanisms, into artifacts that could eventually exhibit the attributes of organisms. In this sense, it is possible to claim that the "biologization" of design is one of the outcomes of the cybernetic imagination of architecture.

The above idea is fundamental to understand the evolution of digital architecture. In the previous pages, the biological trend of digital architecture was barely sketched. So far, I have mentioned some of the main themes and concepts explored by digital architects and the connection of such themes with the informational paradigm. A deeper study of the "biologization" of digital architecture will allow me to trace the cybernetic ascendancy of the dominant visions of architecture and design that are at the crossroads of information technology, informational thinking, and biology. Such a survey also permits to situate the relevance of the cybernetic model for the construction of the explanations of contemporary biology and to understand how, as a result of the triangulation effect, such explanations entered the field of architecture.

In order to complete my picture of the cybernetic ascendancy of the dominant expressions of digital architecture, in the following chapters I will discuss two leading approaches, briefly discussed in the previous pages, that have played a key role in the evolution of the computational perspective in the profession and the "biologization" of design. I refer to the design approaches that, in base of the use of generative design techniques, have advanced bio-inspired conceptions of architecture and design in which architectural objects are constructed as genetic mechanisms and as complex phenomena. From the analysis of the cybernetic ascendancy of genetic and emergent design models, in the next chapters I aim to show how the key ideas about the production of space inherent to the systems view of architecture have materialized in new explanations that involve both the exploration of digital design methodologies, and the imagination of design issues in reference to other scientific fields and theories that make part of the line of thought inaugurated by Wiener and his colleagues.

Notes

1 Kwinter, *Architectures of Time,* 14.
2 Ibid.,14.
3 See in this respect my discussion in Chapter 2 about the connection between the *Performance Design* model and the "utility function" inherent to the logic of the "optimization methods" exposed by Herbert Simon in *The Sciences of the Artificial.*
4 Differently to Systems Analysis, which defines a problem solving approach to design issues and is directly connected to the pragmatics of the computer, as will be seen here, the systemic view of things, as promoted by Systems Theory, offers a more general framework to think of a variety of phenomena in diverse fields as forms of organization based on the interconnection of various elements.
5 See in this respect: Rovaletti, "Teoría general de los sistemas," 45.
6 Von Bertalanffy, *General Systems Theory.*
7 Ibid.
8 For a broad description of the notion of "relationality in the context," see: Rovaletti, "Teoría general de los sistemas."
9 Von Bertalanffy, *General Systems Theory.*
10 Ibid.
11 Ibid.
12 Morin, *Introduction à la pensée complexe.*
13 Ibid.
14 Lazlo. *The Systems View of the World.*
15 Ibid.
16 Ibid.
17 Ibid.
18 Ibid.
19 Dosse, *Histoire du structuralisme,* 492–494.
20 Morin, *Introduction a la pensée complexe,* 28–29.
21 Lafontaine, *L'empire Cybérnetique,* 118.
22 In an influential paper titled "Principles of the Self Organizing System," Ashby defines organisms and machines in terms of the communication between the parts that constitute a whole. The same characterization of natural systems was employed by Maturana and Varela, who promoted a cybernetic description of the organism as a self-organized system, such description that keeps a direct connection to von Bertalanffy's construction of the organism as an open system.
23 See in this respect: Umpleby & Dent, "The origins and purposes of several traditions in systems theory and cybernetics," 80.
24 Von Bertalanffy, *General Systems Theory.*
25 See in this respect: Lafontaine, *L'empire cybernétique.*
26 Grobman & Neuman, *Performalism: a manifesto for architectural performance*, 4.
27 Ibid.,5.
28 Ibid., 4.
29 See in this respect: Schumacher, "Parametricism as style - Parametricist manifesto." See also: Flores, "La autopoiesis de la arquitectura."
30 Schumacher, "Architecture's next ontological innovation," 101.
31 Ibid., 102.
32 Ibid., 104.
33 Ibid., 104.
34 Moe & Smith, "Introduction. Systems, technics and society."

35 Hensel, "Performance oriented design from a material perspective," 43.
36 Hensel & Menges, "Differentiation and performance," 63.
37 Braham, "Biotechniques."
38 Rahim, "Performativity," 182.
39 Crucially, the question of emergence is at the core of systems thinking. This concept describes the appearance in a system of properties that its parts do not possess individually, and that arise due to their interaction (like the collective intelligence of a colony of ants, for instance). This idea was central to von Bertalanffy's work from the early stage of his career. As Jeffrey Goldstein recalls, "Bertalanffy's term for what the British and Americans were calling emergence was «integrations of higher order»," and he used it explicitly to deal with the "issue of to what extent it was justified to consider «supra-individual entities» composed of living organisms as «integrations of higher order» since the former have their own individuality and laws. More generally, Bertalanffy's thesis addressed the issue of whether the world should be understood as a hierarchy of levels of organization, a theme that has been invoked in emergentist circles since the idea was first broached over a century ago." See in this respect: Goldstein, *A review of "The Dialectical Tragedy of the Concept of Wholeness: Ludwig von Bertalanffy's Biography Revisited."*
40 Leatherbarrow, "Architecture's unscripted performance," 16.
41 See in this respect: Picon, *Digital Culture in Architecture.*
42 I refer to the concept of natural system as it is employed by Ervin Lazslo. As mentioned earlier, Laszlo calls "natural systems" all the structures (organic or not) that do not owe their existence to a conscious planning and which display any form of organization that is not the product of agents external to the system.
43 The trend among digital architects to search for sources of inspiration in scientific knowledge is not at all new in architectural practice. Since antiquity, natural sciences have provided architects with a series of images and metaphors that are translated both into architectural discourse and form. In the same way, several scientific paradigms have entered architectural knowledge by means of the adoption of a variety of mechanical and organic models of explanation that have been imagined by scientists to describe a diversity of phenomena and that architects have interpreted in architectural terms.
44 See in this respect: Wiener, *Cybernetics.*
45 Sprecher, "Informationism: information as architectural performance," 27.

Bibliography

Braham, William W. "Biothechniques: Remarks on the Intensity of Conditioning." In *Performative Architecture. Beyond Instrumentality.* Edited by Branko Kolarevic and Ali M. Malkawi, 55–70. New York: Spon Press, 2005.

Dosse, François. *Histoire du structuralisme.* Paris: La Découverte, 1995.

Goldstein, Jeffrey. "A Review of The Dialectical Tragedy of the Concept of Wholeness: Ludwig Von Bertalanffy's Biography Revisited." *Emergence: Complexity and Organization* 11, no. 1 (2009): 113.

Grobman, Yasha J, and Eran Neuman. *Performalism: A Manifesto for Architectural Performance.* Edited by Yasha J Grobman and Eran Neuman. London, New York, 2012.

Hensel, Michael. "Performance-Oriented Design from a Material Perspective: Domains of Agency and the Spatial and Material Organization Complex." In *Performalism: Form and Performance in Digital Architecture.* Edited by Yasha J. Grobman and Eran Neuman, 43–48. New York: Routledge, 2012.

Hensel, Michael, and Achim Menges. "Differentiation and Performance: Multi Performance Architectures and Modulated Environments." *Architectural Design* 76, no. 2 (2006): 60–69.
Kwinter, Sanford. *Architectures of Time: Towards a Theory of the Event in Modernist Culture*. Cambridge, MA: MIT Press, 2001.
Lafontaine, Céline. *L'empire cybernétique. Des machines à penser à la pensée machine*. Paris: Editions du Seuil, 2004.
Laszlo, Ervin. *The Systems View of the World: A Holistic Vision for Our Time*. New York: Hampton Press, 1996.
Leatherbarrow, David. "Architecture's Unscripted Performance." In *Performative Architecture. Beyond Instrumentality*. Edited by Branko Kolarevic and Ali M. Malkawi, 5–20. New York: Spoon Press, 2005.
Moe, Kiel, and Ryan E Smith. "Introduction. Systems, Technics and Society." In *Building Systems: Design Technology and Society*. Edited by Kiel Moe and Ryan E Smith, 1–10. New York: Routledge, 2012.
Morin, Edgar. *Introduction à la pensée complexe*. Paris: Editions du Seuil, 2005.
Picon, Antoine. *Digital Culture in Architecture. An Introduction for the Design Professions*. Basel: Birkhauser GMBH, 2010.
Rahim, Ali. "Performativity: Beyond Efficiency and Optimization in Architecture." In *Performative Architecture. Beyond Instrumentality*. Edited by Branko Kolarevic and Ali M. Malkawi, 177–192. New York: Spoon Press, 2005.
Rovaletti, María L. "Teoría general de los sistemas." *Signo y Pensamiento* 15 (1989): 45–56.
Schumacher, Patrick. "Architecture's Next Ontological Innovation." In *Not Nature, Tarp – Architectural Manual*. New York: Pratt Institute, 2012.
—. "Parametricism as Style-parametricist Manifesto." *11th Architecture Biennale, Venice*, 2008: 17–20.
Sprecher, Aaron. "Informationism: Information as Architectural Performance." In *Performalism. Form and Performance in Digital Architecture*. Edited by, Neuman Eran and Yasha J Grobman, 27–31. London – New York: Routledge, 2012.
Umpleby, Stuart A., and Eric B. Dent. "The Origins and Purposes of Several Traditions in Systems Theory and Cybernetics." *Cybernetics and Systems: An International Journal* 30, no. 2 (1999): 79–103.
Von Bertalanffy, Ludwig. *General Systems Theory*. New York: Georges Braziller, Inc, 1968.
Wiener, Norbert. *Cybernetics or Control and Communication in the Animal and the Machine*. Cambridge, MA: The MIT Press, 1961.

4 Genetic mechanisms

In the precedent chapter, I traced the connection between the systems view in architecture and the emergence of biology as a model of explanation in the productions of digital architecture. I argued that the consolidation of biology as a model in the profession is related to the adoption of the informational description of natural systems, as advanced by systems thinkers, who employed the cybernetic conception of things to explain the functioning of organisms. Importantly, the communicational conception of living systems transcended the explanations of the organism offered by cybernetics and systems theory. As a matter of fact, as a result of the expansion of cybernetic discourses, since the mid twentieth century it has been common in natural sciences to describe different biological phenomena in reference to concepts such as information, programming, message, and code. Behind the expansion of cybernetic narratives in the explanations of biology is a question that merits particular attention in the context of the present study – which aims to assess the influence of cybernetic thinking in the productions of digital architecture. I refer to the close relation that has existed, since the second half of the twentieth century, between computer science and natural sciences.

According to various authors, since the beginnings of computer science the feedback among informatics and biology has been constant, and such feedback has shaped the development of both fields during the last seven decades. In this respect, Hayles argues that the notions of computing have served as a model for biology, at the same time the informational representations of natural systems have informed diverse developments in the field of computer science.[1] This idea is shared by the computer scientist Melanie Mitchell, who claims that the precursors of cybernetics and computer science (among them Norbert Wiener, Alan Turing, and John von Neumann) shared a common ambition, namely, to create intelligent systems, able to imitate the reproductive and adaptive capacities of organisms.[2] For the author of *An Introduction to Genetic Algorithms*, these shared ambitions explain why the first cybernetitians and computer scientists were particularly interested as much in electronics as in biology and psychology. It also explains why they observed natural systems as a model

DOI: 10.4324/9781003181101-4

for their ideas. Interestingly, some groundbreaking experiments in the fields of cybernetics and computer science – such as William Ross Ashby's homeostat, William Grey Walter's tortoises, and von Neumann's automata – were conceived by their creators as artificial mechanisms that allowed them to study and represent their thoughts on the functioning of the organism and the nervous system.[3]

Behind the abovementioned investigations was an idea amply discussed in the academic circles during the early days of informatics; I refer to the conviction, shared by various scientists, that organisms and information processing systems could be considered as analogous forms of organization. This idea, which underlies the development of cybernetics and informatics, was central to the consolidation of the informational conception of biological phenomena. Such paradigm shift in the explanations of biology was in turn, via the triangulation effect, crucial for the emergence of the genetic imagination of architecture. Amply explored by practitioners of digital architecture, genetic design stands out as one of the dominant models of digital architecture. Crucially, it is an approach to design issues that is grounded on architectural interpretations of the informational description of organic processes, such as heredity, evolution, adaptation, and on the informational techniques developed in biology to study and simulate these phenomena.

In accordance with the cybernetic construction of the above-mentioned biological phenomena, digital architects have imagined buildings as sorts of genetic mechanisms. Accordingly, they have fostered design approaches based on descriptions of architectural objects as programmed systems, as adaptive and evolutionary artifacts and as the product of morphogenetic processes. These constructions of architectural issues reinforced the informational epistemology of digital design advanced by the performative and systemic approaches, and they set the ground for several design practices where the technological mediation of architecture has been considered (in line with the ambitions of the fathers of cybernetics and computer science) as a means for architecture to literally achieve biology.

In the following pages, I will sketch the connection among some milestones in the development of the informational paradigm and the consolidation (and further spread) of the cybernetic conception of living systems, as represented by the development of molecular biology and bioinformatics. Drawing from this analysis, I will explain how genetic design models reinscribe the cybernetic conception of architecture in reference to a series of ideas and techniques inherited from the branches of biology that consolidated due to the expansion of the cybernetic imagination of the organism. I will also show how the genetic imagination of architecture has become a preferred space of speculation about the scope of the computerization of the profession, and the stage for the emergence of utopian visions about the autonomy of technologically mediated architecture. Finally, I will show how, despite significant differences of focus between the work of various digital architects, genetic design models are the product of the architectural "ontologization" of the central premise of cybernetic thinking; namely, the idea that all phenomena in the world are in essence information.

Informational thinking, informatics, and biology

The histories about the development of the informational imagination of biology illustrate clearly the connection among informational thinking, informatics, and life sciences referred previously. It is a history that begins when the pioneers of cybernetics and computer science started to imagine artificial systems able to mimic the functioning of natural systems, and when they attempted to explain the functioning of natural systems according to the logic of their inventions. As we will see, the feedback among the informational explanations and the informational simulations of natural systems shaped some of the most powerful metaphors of modern science. More importantly (for what concerns the evolution of digital architecture), such exchanges set the ground for the development of molecular biology – which gave way to the spread of the cybernetic explanations of organic phenomena to other branches of biology. A few anecdotes concerning key developments in the fields of cybernetics and computer science, that recall their connection to biology, permit to situate the emergence of the informational conception of biological phenomena.

One of the paradigmatic examples of the abovementioned feedback among the informational explanations and informational simulations of natural systems appears in Alan Turing's famous paper *On computable numbers*. Turing's article describes a theoretical machine that came to be known as *Turing Machine*, able to read data from a tape that contains a chart of mechanical actions.[4] This system, which was conceived by Turing as a means to prove a fashionable mathematical problem of his time (the decision problem) was also a key development in the history of computer science; till today, the Turing Machine is a preferred model for theorists investigating computation models. Above and beyond its technical contribution to the development of computing, the *Turing Machine* is the embodiment of an idea that shaped the work of Turing and other pioneers of informational thinking and informatics; I refer to the belief that thought is computable. In this sense, the *Turing Machine* must be considered as a formal representation of human thought and a means to create it automatically. By extension, the *Turing Machine* is also the paradigm of one of the most powerful metaphors in the history of modern science, namely, the comparison between the computer and the brain.

In his book, *Une Histoire de l'Informatique*, the sociologist of science Philippe Breton explains that Turing's work had a great impact in the investigations of the neurophysiologist Warren McCulloch, one of the founders of cybernetic thinking.[5] Inspired by the *Turing Machine*, McCulloch took a step forward toward the comparison between the human thought and information processing systems. In collaboration with the logician Walter Pitts, McCulloch imagined a model of the brain as a sort of computing device.[6] This work, known as the McCulloch-Pitts neuron, was determinant for the consolidation of the idea, amply discussed by cybernetitians and computer scientists, that computing machines and the human brain could be considered as analogous systems. More importantly, the model of the brain proposed by McCulloch and Pitts was a key reference in the work of the Hungarian mathematician John von Neumann. According to Breton, von Neumann got to know the work of Turing through the investigations of McCulloch. Subsequently, he created the first digital computer based on the ideas of Turing, and he also published several influential papers that fostered the comparison between computational and natural systems, among them the classic essay, *The Computer and the Brain,* and his investigations about self-replicating automata.

Interestingly, von Neumann's interest in biology was not limited to the comparison between the computer and the brain. Von Neumann's research was also informed by the description of the mechanisms of heredity in organisms as an informational process. This connection appears clearly in von Neuman's ideas about the possibility of creating self-replicating automata. His prominent paper, *The general and logical theory of automata*, describes a theoretical machine that could replicate itself using a series of elemental parts and a set of instructions that the machine could reproduce.[7] In this theoretical machine, the function of the instructions was imagined as a mechanism that mimicked the function of the genes in organisms, while the copy of the instructions was imagined as the action of duplicating the genetic material effectuated by the living cells. Subsequently, von Neumann developed his research on Cellular Automata – a mathematical idealization of physical systems where time and space are considered as discreet factors[8] – as a means to produce an experimental model of the ideas described in *The general and logical theory of automata*. However, the implications of the development of the Cellular Automata model were not restricted to the world of computer science. In the following decades, Cellular Automata would be broadly used as a model to study different problems in biology and more importantly, its development is considered a milestone in the history of bioinformatics. The former comes as no surprise if one takes into account that von Neumann's ambition to create self-replicating machines was inseparable from his interest in biology and especially in genetics. In fact, this research interest would lead him to pay particular attention to the new ideas about genetics in vogue during the postwar period and to dialogue with some of the scientists that at the time worked on informational explanations of the mechanisms of heredity. Crucially, as we will see next, von Neumann's transactions with researchers such as Max Delbrück and Sol Spiegelman constitute a key aspect among the developments which gave birth to molecular biology and bioinformatics.[9]

From the genetic code to bioinformatics

According to Michel Morange's history of molecular biology, this branch of biology resulted from the union of two distinct fields of life sciences: genetics and biochemistry. Morange claims that molecular biology consolidated when hundreds of geneticists started to study the function of the genes, at the same time that biochemists tried to understand the role of genes in the production of proteins and enzymes. In other words, says Morange, molecular biology appeared when genes where linked to a macro-molecule, DNA, and when the structure of DNA was determined and its role in the synthesis of proteins was characterized.[10]

According to the "central dogma" of molecular biology, established by Francis Crick, the genetic material is transcribed into RNA and afterwards translated into proteins. Accordingly, the objective of molecular biology was defined as the study of the processes of replication, transcription, and translation of genetic material in the living cell. As it is explained by Lilly E. Kay, the key idea behind this research objective was the construction of DNA as a code, as a sort of computational program. Of course, this conception of the mechanisms of heredity was inspired by the information discourses, broadly discussed in academic circles during the second half of the twentieth century. According to the informational view of things, Crick explained the synthesis of proteins as the circulation of matter, and mainly of information, from DNA to proteins.[11] Kay argues that, in this way, Crick formalized the informational conception of heredity as a way to impose a new thematic order in which the communicational vision of things fostered by cybernetics was situated at the core of biological research. It was in this context that emerged various informational representations of DNA. Such representations include the description of DNA as a sort of teleological and self-regulated cellular computational program, as the set of instructions that determine the development of the body, and of the living organism as a programmed system, These ideas were promoted by prominent scientists such as Henry Quastler, Carl R. Woose, Jaques Monod, François Jacob, Robert Sinsheimer, and George Beadle, among others. Among the dominant ideas fostered by these researchers are descriptions of heredity as a sort of information processing system and of the genome as a computer; the account of genetic processes as preprogrammed routines; the existence of an internal genomic language in which computations are carried out; the view of biological development as a self-organizing machine; and the description of genetic regulation as a feedback system.[12]

The cybernetic descriptions mentioned earlier for the mechanisms of genetics illustrate clearly the influence of information discourses in contemporary biology. Interestingly, as in some of the examples cited in the previous section, this influence worked in two senses. In this way, computer science became both a receptor and a vehicle of the cybernetic imagination of biology, which eventually transcended the limits of molecular biology. As a matter of fact, the abovementioned work of John von Neumann on self-replicating automata and Cellular Automata (which anticipated the subsequent consolidation of bioinformatics as an independent branch of biology) is the best example of this point. As it was mentioned before, von Neumann's ambition to create self-replicating machines was informed by the work of a series of geneticists who worked on the informational explanation of the mechanisms of heredity. Kay explains that through the interaction with the community of scientists who studied these mechanisms, von Neumann was particularly attracted by the explanation of the relationship gen-enzyme advanced by the microbiologist Sol Spiegelman (Kay reminds that Spiegelman postulated that genes "continually produced, at different rates, partial replicas of themselves that entered the cytoplasm."[13]) While von Neumann found in the work of Spiegelman inspiration for his work, Spiegelman was captivated by von Neumann's ideas about the production of self-replicating machines. So, at the same time that the encounter with the bio-medical community gave von Neumann the confidence to believe that his model corresponded to the actual mechanisms present in natural systems, his work contributed to the consolidation of the informational descriptions of the functioning of heredity that gave birth to molecular biology.[14]

Interestingly, von Neumann's Cellular Automata model (which, as explained before, was conceived as an experimental model of the ideas described in *The general and logical theory of automata*) was further used for the study of different biological problems. Take, for instance, Stephen Wolfram's research presented in *A New Kind of Science,* which constitutes a vast research about the use of Cellular Automata in biology. According to Wolfram, the idea of thinking about the organism in terms of programs is evident due to the assumed similitude among genetic material and a computational program. What is more, Wolfram argues that simple computational programs like Cellular Automata – conceived as a means to materialize through a computational program von Neumann's ideas about self-replicating machines – can reproduce several aspects of natural systems.[15]

From the above it follows that biologists did not see Cellular Automata just as an abstract representation of biological phenomena but as a means to simulate their behavior. In this sense, the Cellular Automata model appears as an important precedent of the field of computational biology. As a matter of fact, the close connection among von Neumann's research and the informational conception of heredity constitutes a key factor that permits to situate the research agenda of molecular biology at the origins of computational biology.

The above is confirmed by various researchers who claim that computational biology stems from the views of the organism inherent to molecular biology. For instance, Paul Hogeweg, one of the main promoters of bioinformatics, has claimed that with the emergence of molecular biology it was acknowledged that the study of the mechanisms that allow living systems to collect, process, store, and use information should be the central research subject of life sciences.[16] According to Hogeweg, in base of the explanations of heredity advanced by molecular biology, scientists now considered that one of the determinant aspects of life is the processing of information in various forms.[17] Several researchers share this opinion, and they see computational biology as a branch of biology that consolidated as a means of studying and simulating natural phenomena, conceived as informational systems.[18] More precisely, according to Hogeweg, bioinformatics was born of the objective of merging the analysis of patterns and dynamic modeling, this as a means to understanding the generation of patterns and data processing at different levels in natural systems.[19]

In line with the abovementioned objective, the development of the field of computational biology involved the creation and application of theoretical and data analysis methods, mathematical modeling systems, as well as computational simulation tools for the study of organic systems. In this way, computational biology restructured the field of biology through the introduction of a series of computational tools[20] among the repertoire of techniques developed in molecular biology. Thus, for bioinformatitians, the result of the abovementioned restructuring was the emergence of a new biology grounded on data analysis that turned the life sciences into a science of information.[21]

The transformation of biology into a science of information is another chapter in the history of the transformations of contemporary knowledge that stem from the expansion of the informational paradigm. The way in which cybernetic idioms ended up redefining the explanations and techniques of biological sciences is an essential part of the history of how notions such as message, information, and feedback permeated our explanations of the world. Among the biological phenomena that were redefined in reference to the cybernetic framework are the mechanisms of heredity, development, evolution, and adaptation in organisms. Crucially, these biological notions have played a key role in the consolidation of a genetic imagination of architecture. These concepts now make part of the explanations of architectural issues advanced by some digital architects, who also adopted some of the techniques developed by the biologists and computer scientists that conceived life sciences as a science of information.

Towards a genetic architecture

As it was discussed in the previous chapters, the conception of architectural objects as the materialization of a set of rules contained in a program has been broadly explored in computer-based architectural practices. This approach has been particularly common among design explorations grounded on the use of algorithmic techniques. This approach is at the core of the work of prominent design researchers, such as William Mitchell, George Stiny, and Kostas Terzedis, who have explored design approaches based on generative processes characterized by the use of programming as a means to produce form and the description of the designed object as a formal system. Although some key explorations of generative design – such as those mentioned earlier – have been informed mainly by concepts of computer science and linguistics,[22] the generative design approaches have been usually constructed in reference to ideas that stem from the informational explanations of biological phenomena. These are the approaches that I call genetic design models, which I will deal with below.

Formerly, I discussed the central role of discourses about the autonomy of architecture in the work of digital architects. Quite often, these discourses have been reflected in the ambition of digital designers to produce autonomous buildings and design processes, and, of course, such ambition has been reinforced by the potential of computing to program self-directed systems. As a matter of fact, this search has directed the agenda of several practitioners of digital design, who have found in generative design models the key for the automation of architecture.

Interestingly, among the narratives underlying genetic design approaches, the most common are the comparison between programing languages and the organic mechanisms of heredity and the conception of natural phenomena as systems that display mechanisms analogue to those of computing. Evidently, these design models have been informed by the central dogma of molecular biology, as well as the investigations of computer scientists, such as John von Neumann, Stephen Wolfram, and John Holland, whose work is in the frontier between informatics and biology. For this reason, several explorations of digital design, grounded on the use of algorithmic design techniques, appear as the architectural expression of the connection among informational thinking, computing, and biology discussed earlier.

In architecture, and other design disciplines, the use of generative methods as a means of production of the designed object has been inseparable of the construction of biological narratives to describe design issues. The above appears clearly in the work of Peter Bentley, whose introduction to *Evolutionary Design by Computers* is a kind of manifesto of the genetic imagination of design. For Bentley, a simple look at the marvels of nature is the best argument to admire the power of evolution to create good designs, be it by means of a natural process or a computer generated method. In accordance with this idea, Bentley fosters a narrative of design based on the comparison between the power of computation and the capacity of nature to create highly complex systems. For instance, Bentley claims that "the most complex and remarkable miracle of design ever created – the human brain – was generated by evolution in nature. Not only is it an astonishing design in its finished form, but equally astonishingly, its huge complexity

Figure 4.1

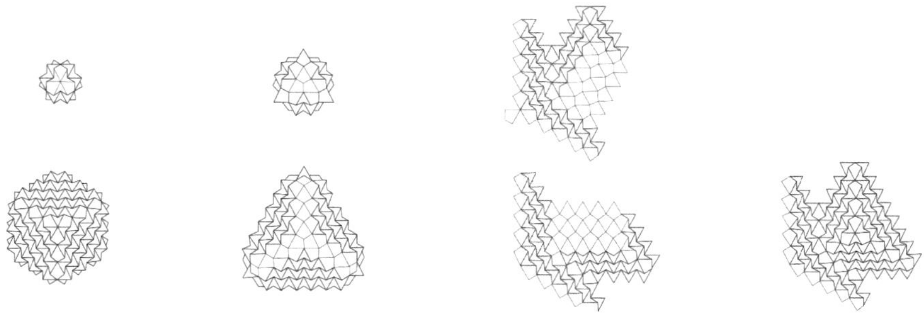

Figure 4.2

grew from a single cell using instructions contained in one molecule of DNA. This is perhaps the most conclusive demonstration of all that the evolution-based techniques of evolutionary computation are highly suitable for design problems."[23]

Following the previous line of reasoning, many digital architects have promoted not only the use of computational techniques in architectural design but an imagination of design issues constructed upon biological metaphors. In this way, they have fostered narratives about architecture and design in which the algorithms that define a generative design process are conceived as the genetic code of buildings, and in which the designs

Figure 4.3

resulting from a computational routine are described as the product of an evolutionary process defined by mechanisms of selection and adaptation.

According to the informational representations of DNA, in genetic design models the architectural objects are conceived as the physical manifestation of a code, as the result of an algorithmic system of genetic variation or as the product of morphogenetic processes.

In this respect, Ingeborg Rocker has referred the emergence of alternative spatial and formal conceptions that "decode and recode architecture."[24] This claim can be interpreted as Rocker's suggestion that the development of new design methods grounded on computational techniques has implied an ontological redefinition of architecture; that is, the replacement of the traditional views of architecture by new conceptions of the disciplinary issues that do not only transform the pragmatics of design, but the whole theoretical apparatus of the profession. Indeed, the genetic conceptions of design advance the same views of architectural problems discussed in the previous chapters. As it will be discussed below, underneath the biological narratives of architecture fostered by genetic design models are the same conceptions of design issues promoted by performative and systemic conceptions of design; namely, the conception of buildings as performative objects, as dynamic agents highly integrated with the context, as self-regulated objects, and, of course, as semi-organic artifacts.

The paradigmatic example of the connection among the genetic conceptions of architecture and the cybernetic imagination of design is the model elaborated by John Frazer, presented in his popular essay *An Evolutionary Architecture*. In Frazer's model – which is grounded on metaphors about the genetic programming and the evolution and the adaptability of architecture – converge computational design techniques, cybernetic constructions of design, and the explanation of architectural problems in reference to biological narratives.

Frazer's description of architecture as a system contained into a program, and its materialization by means of a computational generative process, has important precedents in the work of architects such as Christopher Alexander and Bill Hiller. Both Alexander and Hiller explored design methods based on the study of the dynamic relations among the different elements of a design problem, and they both adopted concepts imported from fields such as linguistics, set theory, systems thinking and computer science to explain the nature of design. But it was when architects like Frazer started to explore the applications in design of techniques inherited from bioinformatics, such as genetic and evolutionary programming, that the informational conceptions of biological phenomena were introduced into the body of knowledge of architecture. When Frazer started to explore the use of techniques such as cellular automata and genetic algorithms in architectural design, at the same time he re-conceptualized design issues in reference to the definition of DNA as a set of rules codified inside the organism, and of morphogenesis as a process directed by the information contained in the genes. In this way, he conceived a computer-based design methodology grounded on the idea that buildings can be considered as evolutionary and adaptive objects; namely, as systems defined by a set of generative rules, which determine, like DNA in living organisms, the evolution and development of the designed object.[25]

For Frazer, these ideas were a means to explore further the systemic view of architecture, which some architects and design researchers in British universities had investigated since the early development of computer science. As a matter of fact, the genetic model of design established by Frazer shares two key aspects of the systemic view of architecture. On the one hand, Frazer's genetic design methods involve an ecologic conception of the built environment, in the broader sense of the term. On the other hand, the genetic view of architecture fosters further the conception of buildings as systems that, like organisms, can be constructed as teleological, sentient, and self-regulated devices.

These ideas about architecture are clearly summarized in the introduction to *An Evolutionary Architecture*, which, significantly, was written by the British cybernetician Gordon Pask.[26] In his introduction to Frazer's book, Pask affirms that the fundamental thesis of the work presented in *An Evolutionary Architecture* is that architecture is a living thing that evolves, and that architecture and the city can be conceived as what emerges from the lives of the dwellers of the built space.[27] These two statements synthesize quite well Frazer's proposal, which fosters a conception of design that aims to introduce in architectural practice two characteristic features of living beings: their capacity to adapt and to evolve. The corollary of this conception of design is a systemic comprehension of the built environment, which implies to consider architecture and the urban space as components of a global ecosystem. These two ideas are explored by Frazer in reference to two biological phenomena, evolution and morphogenesis. In reference to these two concepts, the framework proposed by Frazer is oriented towards the investigation of the fundamental processes of form generation in architecture, this according to the scientific research of the mechanisms of morphogenesis in the natural world. In other words, in Frazer's research, the mechanisms of nature are adopted as a model for the generation of form in architecture. In this sense, the author of *An Evolutionary Architecture* considers architecture as a sort of artificial life that is subject to principles of morphogenesis, genetic coding, replication and selection.[28] In terms of the production of space, in Frazer's work, the above ideas were central to the creation of a design methodology grounded on the production of virtual architectural models able to react to environmental changes. Through the introduction of genetic algorithms as a design tool, Frazer intended to produce in a generative fashion the traditional manifestations of an architectural concept: space, structure and form. In this way, the architectural project, expressed as a set of rules, was conceived as a variable search space based on the evolution and analysis of the designed object.

Of course, the genetic approach to design implied major changes compared to the traditional design methods. The conception of design as a generative computational process implies to transcribe the design intentions into a code, to create a set of rules to control the code, and to translate these rules into a virtual model. In addition, it is necessary to describe the nature of the environment in which the designed object will perform, as well as the selection criteria that define the adaptability of the designed object. Note that this approach advances the same conception of design inherent to performance-based design models. So, according to the genetic view of design, the generative production of space (as a problem of evolution, adaptation, and selection) is analogue to the solution of a design problem by means of the analysis of the performance of the designed object. In fact, in a generative design process rules are defined as instructions for the generation of form, computational models are used to simulate the development of form, forms are evaluated according to their performance, and the evolutionary steps are generated iteratively until a design solution that fits the desired performance is found.

The generative approach to design, in which buildings are defined as adaptive systems that emerge from the rules codified into a computational program, raised as one of the dominant design paradigms of digital architecture. Following this line of research, several contemporary architects have explored similar views of design issues that share two elements of Frazer's model: the use of biological narratives to explain design problems and the development of new design methods grounded on the use of computational techniques that include cellular automata, L-systems, genetic algorithms and multi-agent systems. Among the investigations on this line can be mentioned the work of architects and deign theorists such as Paul Coates, Ingebor Rocker, Michael Silver, Denis Dollens, Karl Chu, and Haresh Lalvani, as well as the influential research of the Emergence and Design Group and the Emergent Design Group. The aforementioned design practices share with Frazer's model a systemic and bio-inspired conception of the built environment, and a vision of architectural space which is grounded both on the exploration of the pragmatics of computing and the construction of metaphors that involve ideas about the genetic codification, morphogenesis, adaptation, and evolution of architecture.

A look at the descriptions of the design research promoted by these architects gives a general idea of the expansion of the genetic view of architecture imagined by Frazer. Take, for instance, Paul Coates' depiction of a design procedure grounded on the use of cellular automata. Coates and his colleagues describe the design process as information codified in the form of transitory states among the cells of a tridimensional matrix. In Coates words, "The cells of the CA resemble those of a natural organism in two respects. First, the behavior and material form of the organism are controlled by instructions encoded identically in all cells in the developing organism. Second, the initial information or genetic structure, expressed in

Figure 4.4

the CA as the combination of initial cell configuration and transition rules set, consists of a series of low level instructions controlling only local transitions between units, requiring a discrete generative mechanism to convert the one dimensional information to three dimensional form."[29]

In the previous example, the rules that define a design appear as the instructions in the genetic code, while buildings are described as organisms constituted by cells. On the other hand, for Coates the result of a design methodology based on genetic programming permits to consider the building as the product of the interaction of its elements at diverse levels. In this sense the building can be considered a self-organized and emergent object and, literally, a form of artificial life.[30]

The description of buildings as living systems has come a long way in the world of genetic architecture. Take, for instance, a conversation between Michael Silver and Evan Douglis (transcribed by Silver in his paper *Codes, eros, and craft*) in which emerge the same themes addressed by Coates. In the cited conversation, Douglis argues that, taking into account the growing knowledge about the functioning of nature and the potential of technology, architecture should define an ambitious research agenda oriented towards the possibility of bringing architecture into life.[31] Along with Douglis, several theorists and practitioners of genetic architecture have fostered narratives about a likely future in which, thanks to the advancement of technology, architecture will eventually achieve biology, buildings

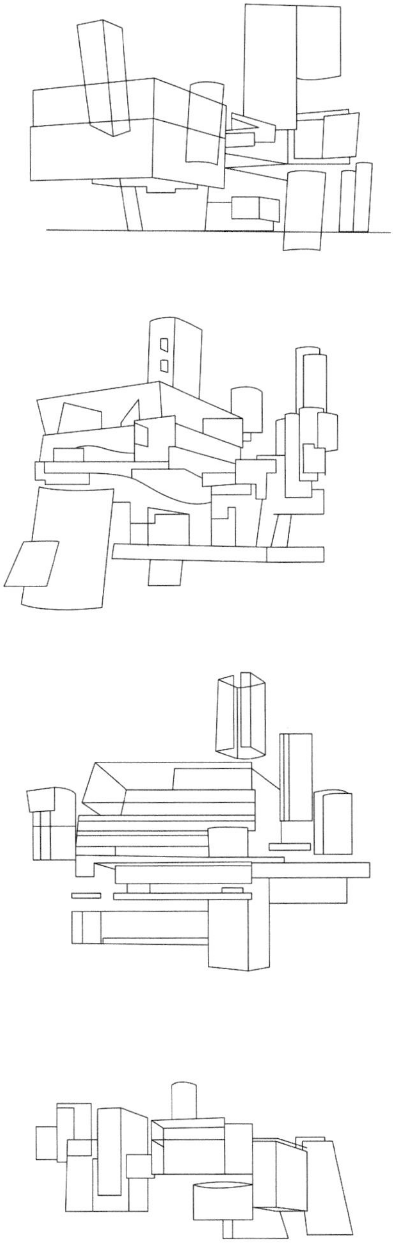

Figure 4.5

will self-reproduce and, consequently, the profession of architecture will disappear.

The utopic turn of genetic architecture

Although Frazer was the first to warn that his ideas about genetic architecture should be understood in a metaphorical sense, the genetic imagination of architecture has become a preferred space of speculation about the possibilities of the "biologization" of design. While in Frazer's model the biological narratives function as a discursive practice that uses scientific concepts to describe a systemic epistemology of computer based design, various contemporary digital architects have pursued prospective visions of a technologically mediated architecture in which the analogies between architecture and biological systems give place to utopian constructions of design issues, and that have taken to another level the ambitions of autonomy of digital architecture.

A good example of this move is the research agenda advanced by Haresh Lalvani, aimed at the production of an architectural genetic map, analogue to the one produced by the *Human Genome Project.* In this respect, Lalvani uses the notion of "morphologic genome" to describe the search of what he calls "the architectural genome," a sort of universal code able to produce any spatial morphology.[32] Thus, in Lalvani's *Genomic Architecture*, the disciplinary problems of architecture are treated as analogue to those of molecular biology; in this sense, the built space is considered a morphological universe composed by an endless set of variations. Accordingly, Lalvani considers computing as a media analogue to the genetic mechanisms of organisms, which offers the means to explore and modify a universe in which every structure, and every kind of architecture, can transform into another into a continuum of space and time.[33]

Lalvani's research is an example of how for some genetic designers the computer is not a tool, but an intelligent machine able to display independent creativity. This idea has allowed digital architects to take to another level the ideas about the autonomy of architecture. For the most enthusiasts, Lalvani included, the technological mediation of the production of space should eventually end up with buildings that design and build themselves from codified forms, processes and materials.[34] Interestingly, when it comes to the genetic imagination of architecture, some of the ideas frequently discussed by digital designers evoke an imagery that competes with the visions of a technologically mediated society advanced by science fiction writers.[35] For example, the idea of attributing to buildings the self-organized and evolutionary character of living beings has been a preferred topic of some utopian explorations of genetic architecture, which have fostered visions of buildings that grow, replicate, and self-organize their own production. This kind of discourse has been taken to the limits of paroxysm by some digital architects who, in line with the ideas exposed in *An Evolutionary*

Architecture, have fashioned architectural fictions that speculate on the possibility of creating literally living buildings thanks to the advances of computing and bio-technologies. Lalvani himself has fostered the vision of a probable future in which buildings will become entirely autonomous entities, putting an end to the profession of architecture. In his own words, when architecture will achieve biology, it will become life and buildings will no longer need architects. In this scenario, the autonomy of organic architecture will imply the end of the profession as we know it today.[36]

Karl Chu, who is undoubtedly the most visible promoter of the utopian trend of genetic architecture, has advanced a similar agenda in his *Metaphysics of genetic architecture and computation*. Like Lalvani, Chu has imagined the combined use of computing and biogenetics to reorganize the world of architecture in base of generative principles; the former by means of the manipulation of what he calls the "hidden reserve of life," that is, the genetic code.[37] Accordingly, Chu situates at the core of his conception of architecture the comparison between computing and the informational nature of organic phenomena. Based on the idea that computer science embodies the human ambition to create intelligent systems and to codify the logic of life, Chu's conception of architecture evokes the informational view of the world exposed by the American scientist John Wheler. According to Wheler, every object in the universe has an immaterial source which is information. This vision of things implies that everything, including physical processes, can be understood as forms of computing. In this respect, the author of *Metaphysics of genetic architecture and computation* claims that the convergence of computer science and biogenetics should lead us to a post-human age in which architecture will emancipate from anthropology. Defined by Chu as "xenoarchitecture," this new architecture will exhibit autonomy and agency, and it will replace the myth of matter for that of information. Paraphrasing Mies van de Rohe's definition of architecture as the art of assembling two bricks together, Chu's idea of generative architecture is the art of putting bits together, bits that are programmed to self-replicate, self-organize, and self-synthetize in new constellations of relations and forms of organization.[38]

Manifestly, Chu's conception of architecture is the translation into architectural problems of von Neumann's ideas about the creation of self-replicating automata. The view of architecture advanced by Chu is mainly inspired by the genetic notion of replication, a concept which, as we have seen, is inherent to the central dogma of modern genetics and a fundamental aspect of computing. In this respect, Chu says that "Implicit within the concept of genetics is the idea of replication of heritable units based on some rule inherent within the genetic code, and embedded within the mechanism for replication is a generative function: the self-referential logic of recursion. Recursion is a function or rule that repeatedly calls itself or its preceding stage by applying the same rule successively, thereby generating a self-referential propagation of a sequence or a series of transformations. It is this logic encoded within an internal principle which constitutes the autonomy of the generative that lies at the heart of computation."[39] Translated into design, this logic is the basis of Chu's idea of an architecture able to design and perpetuate itself, just like the self-replicating machines imagined by von Neumann.

Chu's ideas are of particular interest because, despite its utopian character, they are representative of how the genetic approaches exemplify what could be called the architectural digital zeitgeist; which is nothing other than the trend in digital architecture to rethink the disciplinary problems in reference to the cybernetic idioms inherent to the performative/systemic view of architecture sketched in the previous chapters. As we have seen, from the conception of architecture as a programmed system (a vision that is grounded on the central dogma of molecular biology which defined the construction of DNA as a code), the genetic models endorse the informational vision of design, conceived as an emergent and non-linear process, as well as the conception of buildings as self-regulated and self-organized systems. As a result, they have also endorsed the ambition of digital architects to produce autonomous architectures, this in base of the exploration of design methods that attribute to the built space the presumed informational character of natural phenomena. These common factors show to what extent genetic design models (regardless of whether they promote a utopian vision of architectural issues or not) embraced and fostered the cybernetic imagination of architecture. The centrality of the cybernetic paradigm in genetic design models is particularly evident in the way they have "ontologized" the central premise of cybernetic thinking.

The genetic view and the ontologization of information

Certainly, there are significant differences among the diverse approaches of genetic architecture discussed above. Paraphrasing A. V. Sokolov – who classifies the work of scientists according to their attitude towards the discourses of information – we can claim that while architects like Frazer and Coates stand for the use of information discourses but hold to the

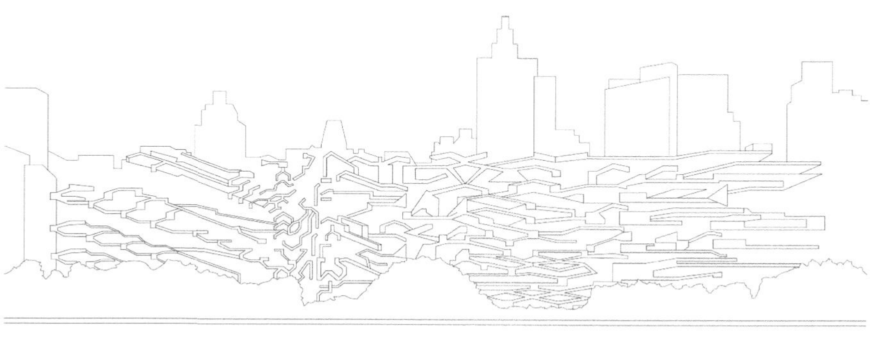

Figure 4.6

traditional problems of architecture, others, like Chu and Lalvani make part of the mythmakers, "who postulate the existence of information as 'the generative source' giving birth to the Macrocosm and other natural and artificial realities."[40]

However, be them mythmakers or not, what is clear is that on the basis of the discourses advanced by genetic designers there is an "ontologization" of the central premise of cybernetic thinking; namely, the idea that all phenomena in the world can be explained in terms of the exchange of information. As we have seen, this idea is on the basis of the transformation of modern biology. Such transformation begun when the mechanisms of heredity in living beings started to be perceived as a sort of informational system, that is, as a system based on the transmission, transcription, and replication of information contained in the genes. Thenceforth, biologists started to study a variety of organic phenomena according to the informational paradigm.

The cybernetic model had already set the ground to think of architectural objects as systems that could display the features of living beings, such as their capacity to adapt, to evolve, and to self-organize their development. With the raise of the informational explanations of heredity, biology provided architects with the theoretical and technical apparatus to consider the production of form as the product of a programmed system. It was in this way that digital architects started to consider that buildings, like organisms, could be subject to principles of genetic programming, replication, and selection. It was possible thanks to the use of computing techniques that emerged themselves from the conception of biological and computational systems as analogue phenomena. By adopting these techniques, digital architects also embraced the idea that the codification of architecture is the ideal means to produce a built environment able to display the features of organisms. In the same way that natural scientists "ontologized" information by making the informational explanations of biological phenomena speak for the reality of organisms, digital architects made the informational imagination of architecture speak for the reality of buildings. It was due to this ontological shift that in genetic design models buildings became programmed, adaptive, and evolutionary systems.

This shift represents an important echelon in the evolution of the cybernetic constructions of architecture. As we have seen, genetic design models re-inscribe both the conception of buildings as dynamic self-regulated systems and the construction of design as a discipline related to the logic of systems analysis. In addition, the conception of buildings as programmable devices gave way to new visions about the autonomy of architecture, in which buildings could eventually form and create themselves. Beyond the utopian agendas associated to this idea, which has proved to be very appealing to digital architects, *it has given place to new investigations that (thanks to advances in fields such as digital fabrication and material science) have introduced the analysis of the material behavior of space into the research agenda of digital architects*. This search is at the core of, some of the most recent explorations of computer-based design, which have found in the ideas of complexity science the paradigm of a radically emergent architecture. This is the subject for the following chapter, in which I will trace the cybernetic ascendancy of the constructions of architecture as a complex system.

Notes

1 Hayles, *How We Became Posthuman*.
2 Mitchell, *An Introduction to Genetic Algorithms*.
3 See, in this respect: Pickering, *The Cybernetic Brain*. In this crucial survey of the evolution of the cybernetic framework, Pickering traces several histories regarding the parallel evolution of cybernetic concepts and information technology.
4 Turing, "On computable numbers."
5 See in this respect: Breton, *Une histoire de l'informatique*.
6 For a full description of the McCulloch-Pitts neuron, see: McCulloch & Pitts, "A logical calculus of the ideas immanent in nervous activity."
7 Von Neumann, *The general and logical theory of automata*.
8 Von Neumann & Burks, *Theory of self-reproducing automata*.
9 See in this respect: Kay, *Who wrote the book of life?*
10 Morange, *Histoire de la biologie moléculaire*, 6.
11 Kay, *Who wrote the book of life?*, 29.
12 Ibid, 24–25.
13 Ibid, 107.
14 Ibid, 107–108.
15 See in this respect: Wolfram, *A new kind of science*. See also: Wolfram, "Statistical mechanics of cellulara autómata."
16 Hogeweg, "The roots of bioinformatics in theoretical biology," 1.
17 Some examples of the informational functioning of organisms would be the accumulation of information throughout evolution, the transmission of information from DNA to intracellular processes, and the interpretation of such information at diverse levels.
18 See in this respect: Trifonov, "Earliest pages of bioinformatics;" Ouzounis & Valencia, "Early bioinformatics;" Searls, "The roots of bioinformatics."
19 Hogeweg, "The roots of bioinformatics in theoretical biology," 2.
20 Such tools include *some techniques, largely used by digital architects, such as genetic algorithms, L-systems, and multi-agent systems*.
21 See in this respect: Lenoir & Alt, "Flow, Process, Fold."
22 The connection between computer-based design approaches and linguistics is an entire chapter of the story of the cybernetic ascendancy of digital architecture that is not covered by this book, but whose comprehension is crucial to see a full panorama of the penetration of informational thinking in architecture.
23 Bentley, "An Introduction to Evolutionary Design by Computers," 5.
24 Rocker, "When code matters," 5.
25 See in this respect: Frazer, *An evolutionary architecture*.
26 In addition to his collaboration with architects like John Frazer and Cedric Price, Gordon Pask is known in the architectural milieu for being the author of an *influential paper titled* "The Architectural Relevance of Cybernetics," published in 1969 in Architectural Design. In the mentioned paper, Pask advances a conception of architecture as an ensemble of active systems that has been embraced by several digital architects, including Frazer.

27 Frazer, *An evolutionary architecture*, 6.
28 Ibid., 9.
29 Coates et al., "The use of Cellular Automata to explore bottom up architectonic rules," 2–3.
30 Ibid.
31 Silver, "Codes, eros and craft," 67.
32 Lalvani, "Genomic architecture,", 117-118
33 See in this respect: Lobell, "The milgo experiment," 58.
34 Ibid, 61.
35 See, in this respect, the analysis proposed by Kolarevic and Parlac in: *Building dynamics: exploring architecture of change*. See also: Kolarevic "Architecture of Change."
36 Lalvani, "Genomic architecture,", 124
37 Chu, "Metaphysics of genetic architecture and computation."
38 Ibid., 42.
39 Ibid., 45.
40 Sokolov, "Ontology of information."

Bibliography

Bentley, Peter. "An Introduction to Evolutionary Design by Computers." In *Evolutionary Design by Computers*. Edited by Peter Bentley, 1–73. San Francisco: Morgan Kaufmann, 1999.

Breton, Philippe. *Une Histoire De l'informatique*. Paris: La decouverte, 1990.

Chu, Karl. "Metaphysics of Genetic Architecture and Computation." *Architectural Design* 76, no. 4 (2006): 38–45.

Coates, Paul, N. Healy, C. Lamb, and W.L. Voon. "The use of cellular automata to explore bottom up architectonic rules." Proceedings of the "Eurographics UK Chapter 14ht annual conference." Londres: Eurographics Association UK, 1996.

Frazer, John. *An Evolutionary Architecture*. London: Architectural Association, 1995.

Hayles, N. Katherine. *How We Became Posthuman: Virtual Bodies in Cybernetics, Literature and Informatics*. Chicago: The University of Chicago Press, 1999.

Hogeweg, Paul. "The Roots of Bioinformatics in Theoretical Biology." *PLoS Computational Biology* 7, no. 3 (2011): 1–5.

Kay, Lily E. *Who Wrote the Book of Life? A History of the Genetic Code*. Stanford, CA: Stanford University Press, 2000.

Kolarevic, Branco. "Architecture of Change: Building Dynamics and Kinetic Matter." Grenoble: Les Grands Ateliers, 2012.

Kolarevic, Branko, and Parlac, Vera. *Building Dynamics: Exploring Architecture of Change*. Routledge, 2015.

Lalvani, Haresh. "Genomic Architecture." In *The Organic Approach to Architecture*. Edited by Debora Gans and Zehra Kuz, 115–126. Chichester: Wiley-Academy, 2003.

Lobell, John. "The Milgo Experiment: An Interview with Haresh Lalvani." *Architectural Design* 76, no. 4 (2006): 52–61.

Lenoir, Timothy, and Alt Casey. "Flow, Process, Fold." In *Architecture and the Sciences. Exchanging Metaphors*. Edited by Antoine Picon and Alessandra Ponte, 314–353. Princeton, New Jersey: Princeton Architectural Press, 2003.

McCulloch, Warren S, and Pitts Walter. "A Logical calculus of the Ideas Immanent in Nervous Activity. The Bulletin of Mathematical Biophysics." *The Bulletin of Mathematical Biophysics* 5, no. 4 (1943): 115–133.

Mitchell, Melanie. *An Introduction to Genetic Algorithms*. Cambridge, Mass: The MIT Press, 1996.

Pickering, Andrew. *The Cybernetic Brain: Sketches of Another Future*. Chicago: University of Chicago Press, 2010.

Rocker, Ingerborg M. "When Code Matters." *Architectural Design* 76, no. 4 (2006): 16–25.

Silver, Mike. "Codes Eros and Craft: An Interview with Evan Douglis." *Architectural Design* 76, no. 4 (2006): 62–71.

Sokolov, A.V. "Ontology of Information. Philosophical Essays." *Scientific and Technical Information Processing* 37, no. 3 (2010): 149–171.

Trifonov, Edward N. "Earliest Pages of Bioinformatics." *Bioinformatics* 16, no. 1 (2000): 5–9.

Turing, Alan. "On computable numbers, with an application to the Entscheidungs problem." *Proceedings of the London Mathematical Society*. 1937: 230–265.

Von Neumann, John. *The General and Logical Theory of Automata*. Vol. 5, In *Collected Works*. Edited by A H Taub. 1963.

Von Neumann, John, and Arthur, W Burks. *Theory of Self-Reproducing Automata*. Vol. 1102024. Urbana: University of Illinois press, 1966.

Wolfram, Stephen. *A New Kind of Science*. Champaign: Wolfram Media, 2002.

Wolfram, Stephen. "Statistical Mechanics of Cellulara Autómata." In *Cellular Automata and Complexity: Collected Papers*. Reading, MA: Addison-Wesley, 1994.

5 Complex phenomena

Today, five decades after the publication of the special issue about *Performance Design* in *Progressive Architecture,* it is still quite common among architects to think of buildings as performative devices; that is, as objects whose behavior is considered to prevail over traditional conceptions of space related to matters of function, firmness, and beauty. For the theorist of architecture Neal Leach, the architectural tradition that privileges the performance of the building over its appearance is connected to what the French philosopher Gilles Deleuze calls "intensive thinking."[1] It is a mode of thought, described in *Difference and Repetition,* that considers phenomena in terms of forces flows and processes. In Deleuze's words, *intensity* is the productive force of *difference,* that is, the processes that produce the extended and qualified objects of experience.[2]

A useful example of an *intensive* process is the formation of the embryo. As explained by Dale Clisby, "In the development of the embryo we find the distinctive relations between the virtual and the actual as defined by the dual processes of individuation and actualization. The virtual idea corresponds to genetic potentiality. The development of the biological form contains the virtual, genetic potential within it, as *imminent.* This potential determines the lines along which the actual organism forms. *Will this limb bud form into a hand or a wing?* This biological formation depends on a prior field of intensity, both as the environment in which it is formed and as the constitutive elements of its own development."[3] According to the former description, *intensities* can be described as the processes that produce energy, that move the world, and which promote change. The philosopher Manuel De Landa summarizes this idea when he claims that intensive thinking is to think in terms of the critical thresholds that produce morphogenetic events.[4]

In the world of science, complexity thinking is particularly representative of the intensive mode of thought described by Deleuze. As a matter of fact, it is a scientific model that deals with the study of phenomena that can be described in terms of the flux, the change, the formation and dissolution of patterns. Complexity thinking consolidated during the 1980s, and it was born of the efforts of a group of prominent scientists interested in studying

DOI: 10.4324/9781003181101-5

from the same perspective a series of phenomena in different areas that included physics, economy, biology, and computer science. More precisely, these researchers were interested in the study of isomorphic phenomena that they defined as complex systems. Such systems are characterized by being arrangements composed of several elements whose interactions bring into being complex forms of organization (such as the Earth's global climate, the human brain, and social organizations) that display emergent and self-organizing properties. Not surprisingly, complexity science is one of the numerous frameworks that emerged during the second part of the twentieth century in accordance with the research agenda established by the cybernetic paradigm.

As discussed in the previous chapters, since the dawn of the computational perspective in the profession, digital architects have been thrilled by the idea that the architectural object can be understood as an emergent and self-organized phenomenon. Indeed, several recent investigations of digital architecture have pursued this particular idea through explorations of design that I call here emergent design models. Such models describe design methodologies that, in accordance with the cybernetic framework, include the conception of buildings as the spatial and material properties that arise from the dynamic relations among different factors that define an architectural reality. These models explore a praxis of design that is (in a certain way) the continuation of the generative investigations of genetic architecture. They share with genetic design models the conception of architectural form as a programmed system. However, emergent design models have found their main conceptual and technical references not in modern genetics but in complexity thinking, a framework that has provided digital architects with new concepts to think of the morphogenesis of architecture as a material system.

In this chapter I aim to trace the connection between complexity thinking and the elaboration of emergent conceptions of architectural issues and how these constructions of architecture fit into the tradition of cybernetic thinking in digital architecture. For this purpose, in the first part of the chapter I will present a look at the central ideas fostered by complexity science and their connection to the cybernetic paradigm. Subsequently, I will show how the development of emergent design approaches has been informed by the core ideas and concepts of complexity science. This move has permitted digital architects to imagine computer-based formation processes which mimic the generation of a complex system and which evoke the conception of biological development as a material system that displays procedures analogous to computation. Finally, I will show to what extent the construction of design issues in reference to complexity notions evoke the same themes inherent to the performative, systemic and genetic explanations of digital architecture discussed in the previous chapters. In this sense, I consider the construction of architecture as a complex phenomenon as the latest manifestation of the cybernetic imagination of architecture that has been at the core of the evolution of the computational perspective in the profession.

Complexity thinking

Although complexity thinking consolidated as an independent framework during the late twentieth century, its origins can be traced back to a series of scientific developments that took place in the United States after world war II. In fact, some authors consider the publication by Warren Weaver[5] in 1949 of the paper *Science and Complexity* the founding act of complexity science. In *Science and Complexity,* Weaver sketched what would become the fundamental subject of complexity science. He explained that for the study of certain phenomena, the main issue was not the number of variables to analyze but the fact that such variables were interconnected. The kind of phenomena that Weaver referred to, were those that involve a great number of factors organized into an organic whole. Defined by Weaver as problems of organized complexity, such phenomena include all the systems composed of several elements that follow specific rules, and whose interactions produce a pattern of organization over time.[6]

Steven Johnson, author of the popular science book *Emergence: The connected lives of ants, brains, cities and software,* considers that the ideas promoted by Weaver represent a paradigm shift in science that resulted from various epistemological and technological developments. Among such developments can be mentioned Claude Shannon's communication theory, Norbert Wiener's cybernetic theory, Edward O. Willson's studies of ants, Olliver Sigfried's research on artificial intelligence, and John Holland's studies on emergence and adaptation.[7] In base of these developments, complexity science began to take shape at the beginning of the 1980s. Thanks to an initiative of the physicist George Cowan, a group of prominent scientists – that included Stirling Colgate, Nick Metropolis, Herb Anderson, Darragh Nagle, Peter Caruthers, Richard Slansky, and others – joined efforts to create a space of interdisciplinary research based on a new scientific paradigm. Cowan's idea was to create a research center based on a holistic conception of science and on the use of computing for the study of complex phenomena; such project materialized a few years later with the creation of the *Santa Fe Institute* and the consolidation of complexity thinking as a well-defined scientific field.

According to M. Mitchell Waldrop, the objective of complexity science was to define general laws to explain different isomorphic phenomena in base of the advances in fields such as neural networks, artificial intelligence, ecology, and chaos theory. The main interest of this new science was to study natural or artificial phenomena whose main characteristics are to be composed by several simple elements, which interact among them without the intervention of an organism of central control, and whose interaction produces complex forms of organization.[8] At this point it is quite clear that at the core of the abovementioned research interest are three aspects that complexity thinking shares with the systemic view of things fostered by Ludwig von Bertalanffy: the conception of phenomena as systems, the establishment of a research agenda based on the study of the isomorphisms among different phenomena and more importantly, the departure from the tradition of linear thinking that dominated western science until the mid-twentieth century.

For Waldrop, the study of the non-linear dynamics observable in certain systems confronted scientists to the fact that complex phenomena, differently to linear systems, are organized totalities that are bigger than the sum of their parts; that is, they are arrangements of elements that as a whole present higher levels of organization than they do individually.[9] Accordingly, the main question that led the research agenda of complexity thinking was how the world, despite its natural tendency to entropy, is the stage of creation of multiple organized systems able to organize their own structure through the interaction among their components at different levels. In accordance with this question, the research objects of complexity science include a variety of phenomena such as the capacity of cells to produce life, the interconnection of neurons to produce thought and consciousness, the production of physical complex behavior, and the spontaneous organization of systems such as galaxies, stars and hurricanes, and computing. The inclusion of computing as a research object is due to the fact that the study of complex phenomena grew hand in hand with the capacity of computers to make vast amounts of calculations and to analyze problems that are not static structures but patterns that develop in time.[10] For this reason, computer science became a key field in the research agenda of complexity science. But, more importantly, for complexity thinkers computing is an intermediary field among theoretical and experimental sciences that allows researchers to see their equations (theories) displaying patterns (experiments) that otherwise could not be predicted. In other words, in complexity science computing is not just considered a powerful tool to study complexity, it is a field of research connected to the problems of complexity. For instance, for Murray Gell-Man the idea of studying phenomena that could be modeled thanks to computing did not respond exclusively to the fact that the computer allows to simulate complex phenomena, but to the consideration of the computer itself as an example of the object of study of complexity thinking, that is, a complex system.[11] A wider description of the notion of complex system offers a brief overview of the main ideas of the complexity paradigm.

Complex systems

As mentioned earlier, complex systems are phenomena composed by numerous connected components whose interaction produces complex forms of organization. They are systems in which matter, energy, and information interact in complex cycles, as it is the case, for instance, of cities and the nervous system. Another characteristic of complex systems mentioned above is its dependency on the interaction among simple elements from which emerge totalities that are more than the sum of the individual parts that conform the system.[12] For complexity thinkers, it is the richness of the interactions among the elements of complex systems what allow them to achieve spontaneously high organization levels. Indeed, this is one of the essential aspects of complex systems, namely, their capacity to auto-organize their behavior, which guarantees their existence independently of the existence of a hierarchic control system; think, for instance, of an ecosystem.

From the previous, it follows that a given phenomenon is considered a complex system if it is the result of the interaction among a group of elements which, thanks to their exchanges, transcend their individual character and acquire collective properties, like ant colonies and the brain, for instance. In addition, and thanks to their auto-organizing properties, complex phenomena are adaptive and dynamic systems able to make work the conditions of the context in their advantage.[13]

The above features of complex systems are clearly explained by John Holland in his book *Hidden Order: How Adaptation Builds Complexity.* According to Holland, complex phenomena can be described by four general principles. First, complex systems are composed by elements whose interactions can be described as rules. Second, the elements of a complex system can adapt to changing conditions by changing their rules trough the accumulation of experiences. Third, since the environment of a complex system is constituted by other dynamic adaptable systems, the adaptation efforts of a complex system are efforts to adapt to other adaptable systems. In consequence, the fourth principle declares that the patterns that produce a complex system are in permanent change.[14]

Holland's four principles of complex systems summarize quite well the central ideas of complexity thinking. At the core of Holland's principles, we find, in the first place, the definition of the research subject of complexity science (complex systems) as phenomena that arise from the rule directed interaction of the elements of a system; second, the consideration of the result of the interactions between the elements of the complex system as a self-organized process; third, the idea that complex systems make part of a network of systems, so that they must permanently adapt to (and co-evolve with) a changing environment (composed of several adaptable systems). In reference to these ideas, complexity thinkers have developed an interdisciplinary research agenda which involves various fields that include economy, biology, and computer science.

As discussed before, the fundamental premise of complexity thinking is that complex phenomena arise from the interaction of simple elements. In other words, complex systems are emergent and self-organized phenomena. Here appear two crucial considerations that complexity thinkers share with systems thinkers. The first is that, since organized wholes have distinctive properties that are the product of the interaction among different organization levels, the properties of a complex system cannot be deduced form the individual analysis of its parts in isolation. The second is that, a complex system can be simultaneously a form of organization defined by the interaction among simple elements and a component of a system in a higher level of organization. Therefore, complex systems are hierarchic structures of growingly complexity levels.

An example frequently cited to explain the self-organized, emergent and hierarchic configuration of complex systems is the form of organization displayed by the communities of social insects. The ant colony is the paradigmatic example of a system, composed by simple elements, which displays a bottom-up form of organization. In the ant colony, the rule based coordinated actions of a group of individuals gives rise to a highly organized phenomenon. In this kind of organization, the local actions of individual agents produce a more complex global behavior, namely, the colony.[15] The ant colony is also a good example of another aspect of complex systems, that is, its dynamic character. For complexity thinkers, the dynamic character of complex phenomena is central to two interconnected ideas: first, the consideration of emergent behavior as the outcome of transition phases and, second, the conception of emergent systems as feedback systems.

The notion of "transition phase" describes the moment in which a system is able to produce a form of organization that is complex enough so that the system can be considered a self-organized and adaptive system. According to Chris Langton, a leading scientist in the field of artificial life, what distinguishes self-organized adaptive systems is precisely their ability to achieve a high organization level without losing their identity. That is the reason why Langton defines complex phenomena as systems in "the edge of chaos" (a concept that describes the complex behavior as an intermediate point between systems that display a very static form of organization and systems whose organization is very chaotic). For complexity thinkers, the balance between chaos and order in complex systems is possible because complex phenomena display different types of circular causality. According to Holland's principles, complex phenomena are systems composed by elements whose interaction gives rise to complex organization levels that can adapt and co-evolve with other systems. In other words, complex systems can obtain information from their surroundings and adapt their behavior to a changing environment.

From the previous, it follows that the study of complex systems implies to consider them as phenomena that are regulated by mechanisms of negative and positive feedback. Indeed, for complexity thinkers the self-organized behavior of complex phenomena is the outcome of two-way connections that produce higher organization levels. According to Holland, complex systems self-organize by means of the constant revision of their constructive elements. In a general way, these processes are the same in diverse systems, and they are grounded on the same strategy: the permanent feedback among the elements of the system.[16] Evidently, at the core of the complexity view is an idea that has been around since the publication of Norbert Wiener's *Cybernetics* in 1948. I refer to the idea that information processing is present at all levels in nature and that life and computing display similar mechanisms.

The cybernetics of complexity thinking

As we have seen, some of the key aspects of complexity thinking provide clear evidence of the influence of the cybernetic model in this field of knowledge. Among such aspects can be mentioned the connections between complexity theory, operations research, and systems thinking, the exploration of a line of research based on the comparison between computing and life, and especially, the description of emergent and self-organized behavior as the outcome of feedback mechanisms.

Previously in this book, I have argued that the cybernetic notion of circular causality and the representation of phenomena as communicational processes are the basis of several influential developments in contemporary knowledge; of course, such developments include the lines of research promoted by complexity thinkers. According to Manuel De Landa, the techniques that gave rise to the concept of circular causality are on the basis of the emergence of complexity theories. He claims that when Wiener and the engineers involved in the development of radar technology introduced in their research the notion of negative feedback, they became the pioneers of non-linear thinking in western science.[17]

The study of complex phenomena as reciprocal causality systems, as negative and positive feedback systems, is only one of many aspects that explain the connection among cybernetic thinking and complexity science. In fact, all the core ideas of complexity thinking (self-organization, emergence, adaptation) were directly imported from the cybernetic model.[18] For instance, the notion of self-organization was inherited from the work of William Ross Ashby, the investigations of Stuart Kauffman were deeply informed by the work of Warren McCulloch, and Claude Shannon's information theory was key to explain the phenomenon of organized complexity as described by Warren Weaver. Moreover, various key promoters of the complexity framework were formed under the cybernetic paradigm; the economist William B. Arthur was educated in the field of operations research, while John Holland and Oliver Selfridge were students of Norbert Wiener.

For the above reasons, it comes as no surprise that some key scientific developments connected to the rise of cybernetics (automata theory, neural networks, operations research, systems theory, and self-organization theories) make part of the precedents that helped to shape the complexity view. For instance, the thinkers of complexity enriched their comprehension of the notion of organized complexity thanks to the work of McCulloch and

Pitts on neural networks and John von Neumann's investigations about self-replicating automata (which describe systems that function through operations that can be understood in abstract terms as a set of inputs, outputs, and operation rules). These investigations were a crucial influence in the work of some of the main researchers associated with the *Santa Fe Institute*, among them Stuart Kauffman, Stephen Wolfram, and Chris Langton.[19]

With respect to the influence of operations research and systems thinking, the multidisciplinary and holistic approach of the first was, according to Weaver, a crucial factor to deal with problems of organized complexity, while the systems view contributed to the conceptualization of different types of phenomena as isomorphic systems. As a matter of fact, some authors suggest that there is a high degree of conceptual superposition among systems thinking and complexity thinking; in both fields, several concepts have practically the same definition, and the two models share the idea that there are universal principles that underlie all systems.[20]

Concerning the theories of self-organization, it was already mentioned that the concept was coined by William Ross Ashby, who used it to explain dynamic systems' tendency to equilibrium; for Ashby, the balance among the different elements of a system is the result of the mutual dependency among them. This idea, as we have seen, is at the core of the description of complex systems as phenomena resulting from the exchanges among individual elements that, due to their interactions, acquire collective properties. In addition to the work of Ashby, other influential theories of self-organization have influenced the work of complexity thinkers, among them von Neuman's work on self-replicating automata and Heinz von Foerster's, Humberto Maturana, and Francisco Varela investigations about the mechanisms of self-organization.[21]

In connection with the abovementioned antecedents, complexity science defined a research agenda that revisits the core ideas of cybernetic thinking, fostering further the conception of things as organized systems and as communicational phenomena. Crucially, some of the most recent explorations of digital architecture have revisited the cybernetic imagination of design issues by means of the introduction in architectural practice of a set of concepts inherited from the complexity view. From the conception of architecture as a complex phenomenon, these explorations have fostered further the construction of architectural objects as performative, sentient, self-regulated, and semi-organic devices.

Architecture as a complex system

Today, it is quite common among design professionals to think that to solve a design problem is to solve a complex problem.[22] This idea has made a long way in architectural practice, particularly among digital architects. The above comes as no surprise if one takes into account that the complexity paradigm relies heavily on the use of computing and makes part of a systems thinking tradition in science, two aspects that have played a key role in the evolution of digital architecture. As a matter of fact, in the context of the expansion of the cybernetic framework, the construction of architectural issues in reference to the conceptual and technical apparatus of complexity science appears as the logical evolution of a field like digital architecture, in which, as pointed out by Leach, Turnbull and Williams, the conception of design as a problem of control, pre-programming, and centralization has been replaced by its construction in reference to notions such as autonomy, emergence, and distributed functioning.[23]

In recent years, the aforementioned conceptions of design have found a fertile field of exploration both in the techniques employed for the study and simulation of complex phenomena and the intensive ontology of complex emergent systems. However, the construction of architectural objects as the product of emergent processes has not been exclusive of the design practices informed by complexity thinking. As it was discussed in the previous chapter, different design models that have explored generative formation processes are grounded on descriptions of architecture and design as emergent systems. This is the case, for instance, of design approaches that investigate the use of shape grammars, which explore notions of design informed by structuralism and linguistics. The same can be said of genetic design models, which are grounded on informational representations of biological phenomena such as heredity, evolution, and adaptation. In general terms, the very idea of performance involves an emergent conception of architecture, since it implies that any spatial reality is the product of varied dynamic relations. Indeed, this is the common theme of a variety of explorations of digital architecture, which share the consideration of architectural objects as the product of the dynamic interaction between different elements. In the words of Christian Derix, such design explorations consider architecture as objects whose visual and spatial qualities cannot be explicitly authorized by geometrical representation; on the contrary, they consider space as the result, unknown in advance by the designer, of the systemic relations among elements and mechanisms present in a given context.[24]

In line with the ontology of design described by Derix, several practitioners of computer-based design have found in the complexity view the tools to explore further the systemic character of architecture. In reference to the concepts of complexity thinking, emergent design models explore further the conception of architectural objects as systems composed of multiple elements whose interactions give rise to unexpected results. Although the former is, roughly speaking, the same conception of architecture advanced by the cybernetic constructions of design that digital architects have been exploring since the dawn of the computational perspective in architecture, emergent design models constitute a clearly defined line of research based on unique theoretical and methodological tools that have been employed to redefine the question of the morphogenesis of architectural space.

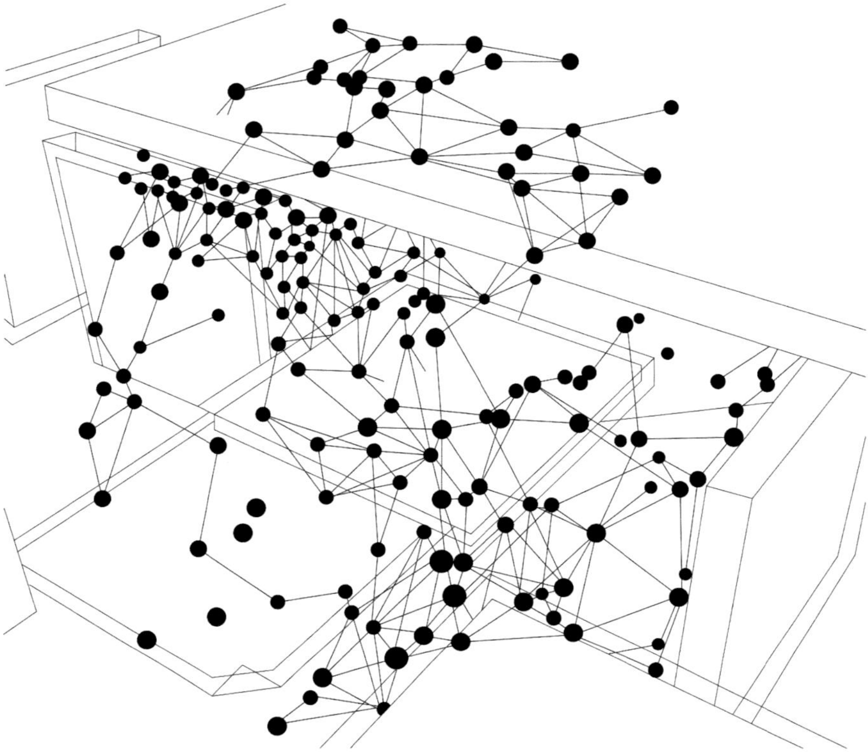

Figure 5.1

At the core of emergent design approaches are the two central themes of complexity thinking. On the one hand, architectural objects are conceptualized as complex systems, that is, as what emerges from the local simple interactions among the elements involved in a given design problem. Accordingly, the elements that make part of the definition of a spatial reality are considered as active agents. In other words, buildings are considered emergent and self-organized systems. According to these two fundamental principles of complex systems, emergent design models explore the possibility to produce complex architectural spaces that arise from the definition of a bottom-up design logic. In recent investigations of digital architecture grounded on the complexity paradigm, the exploration of this bottom-up logic involves the consideration of the material behavior of the designed object a main input for the generation of architectural form. In this respect, emergent models have also explored two ideas broadly discussed by complexity thinkers: the conception of biological development as a physical self-organized process and the conception of computation as a process that is present at all levels in nature. Naturally, the exploration of these ideas has involved the development of design methods that involve the tools employed by complexity thinkers. These tools include computational techniques imported form fields such as computational biology and artificial life, and in some cases, the advances in fields such as material science and bio-mimetic engineering.

Emergent and self-organized form

According to the definition of complex behavior, as the product of the local, simple and non-linear interactions between the elements of a system, digital architects have imagined generative design procedures grounded on the idea that buildings can be programmed to emerge as the result of adaptive and self-organizing properties. That is to say that the architectural object can be conceived as the outcome of the properties that arise from the dynamic relations between the different elements and factors that define a design problem. Accordingly, emergent design processes are based on the identification of the elements that define an architectural reality, of their properties and their interactions. This is, for instance, the base of the design research developed by the *Emergent Design Group*, which investigated the introduction into the design process of a series of techniques and concepts inherited from the field of artificial life.

Artificial life is a field of research established at the *Santa Fe Institute* by Chris Langton, based on the study of computing and life as analogue phenomena. Accordingly, the *Emergent Design Group* developed a design approach based on the consideration of each aspect of a design problem, including environmental aspects, an active component. From this perspective, design is defined as a system in which each element of the system can

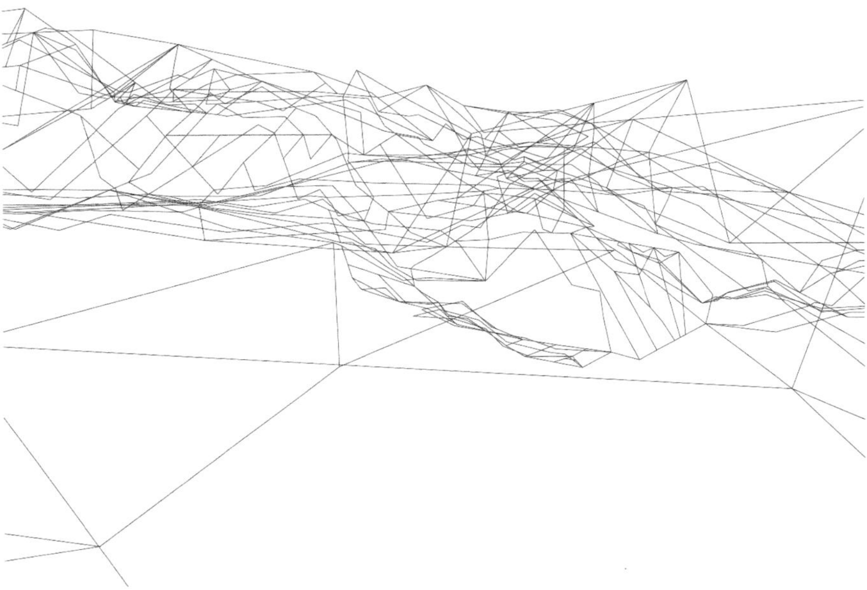

Figure 5.2

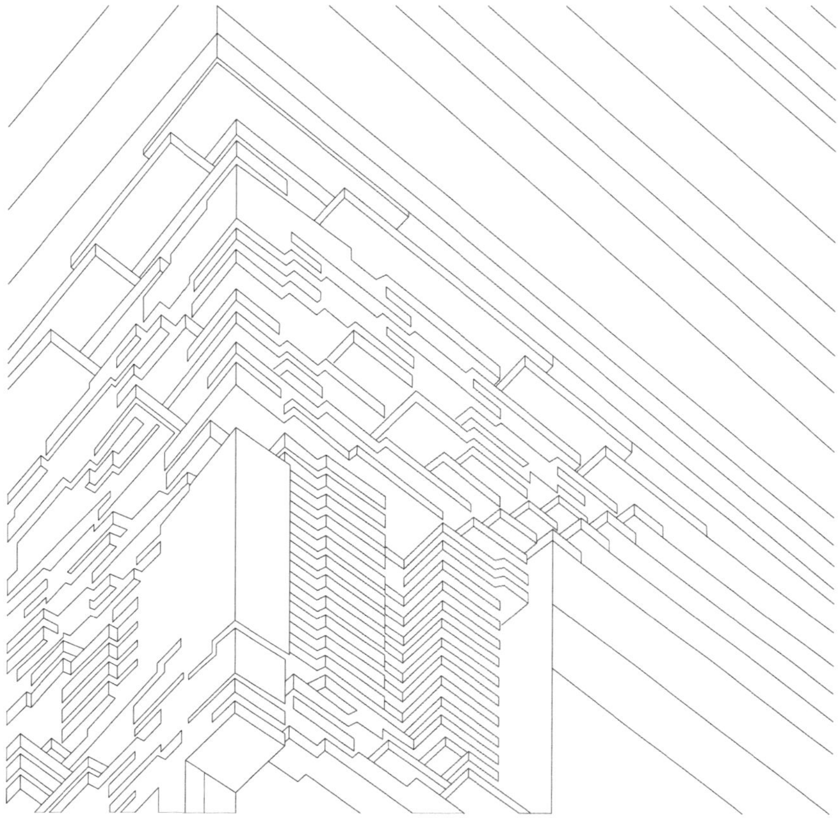

Figure 5.3

affect other elements and the environment, so that the interactions among the components of the system can produce a growingly complex form of organization.[25]

The design logic described above is at the core of different computer-based design practices, where the self-organizing capacity of complex phenomena is explored as a generative force to produce a design. For this reason, emergent design methodologies are grounded on the use of computing techniques, such as cellular automata and agent based systems, which allow designers to produce spatial arrangements that emerge from the rule based interaction among active elements. A good example of this kind of approach is Michael Silver's project *Automason 1.0*.[26] Through the definition of a design strategy based on the use of cellular automata, Silver's *Automason* constitutes a self-organized design system in which the rule-based interaction among the constructive elements of a building produces the global form of the architectural object. Consider how in the description of this system, Silver translates into architectural language the main ideas of complexity thinking. Silver says that by using simple programs "building details obtain their complexity for free: no external agency or extraneous system is needed to design them. This kind of complexity is not dependent on the incessant differentiation of parts, but on the application of fixed rules in a discrete system that requires only two components."[27]

In complexity thinking, the notion of self-organization explains the teleological character of organic systems and other biological phenomena, such as the development of organisms and the emergence of intelligent behavior. Not surprisingly, the construction of the design process as a self-organized system in emergent design practices has resulted in the production of new biological metaphors of architecture, which have fostered further the "biologization" of architecture advanced by several digital architects. As a matter of fact, a common strategy employed by emergent designers is to observe the forms of organization of natural systems to extract rules that can be applied to design problems.

For example, through the exploration of concepts of emergence and self-organization, some digital designers have sought to define design processes that exhibit forms of intelligence of their own. This idea has been broadly explored in emergent design models. The premise is that if the architectural project is defined through the action of agents that adapt to the changes in their local environment, the variables of a design can be processed automatically to acquire an intelligent behavior; it is assumed that as long as there is a group of highly interconnected elements, the emergence of a growingly complex behavior is inevitable.[28] Consider, in this respect, the design research exposed by Benjamin Aranda and Chris Lasch in *Tooling*. Starting with the examination of the simple rules that describe the complex behavior of different natural systems, Aranda and Lasch explore the creation of formal systems that supposedly exhibit the high organization levels of natural systems.[29] Indeed, for Aranda and Lasch, design is analogous to the spontaneous creation of natural systems. Accordignly, in their work the creation of space is similar to the creation of an organized system: once one sets the initial conditions, the production of form goes its own way. In this respect, the authors of Tooling say that "before ideas coalesce into a definite form there must exist some undifferentiated state free of any organization. The moment any sort of development is imposed onto this formless matter it begins to enter the realm of substance, organization, and material."[30] As systems designers, the work of architects is to define the rules for the emergence of a spatial reality out of the elements that compose it (elements which exist as formless matter before they become architecture).

In my opinion, the above description of the formation of space is the best example of the construction of architectural issues according to the complexity view. From the perspective of complexity thinking, the production of architecture is related to the exploration of the forces that influence the movement of a design idea from a pre-material state to the realm of the material.

Figure 5.4

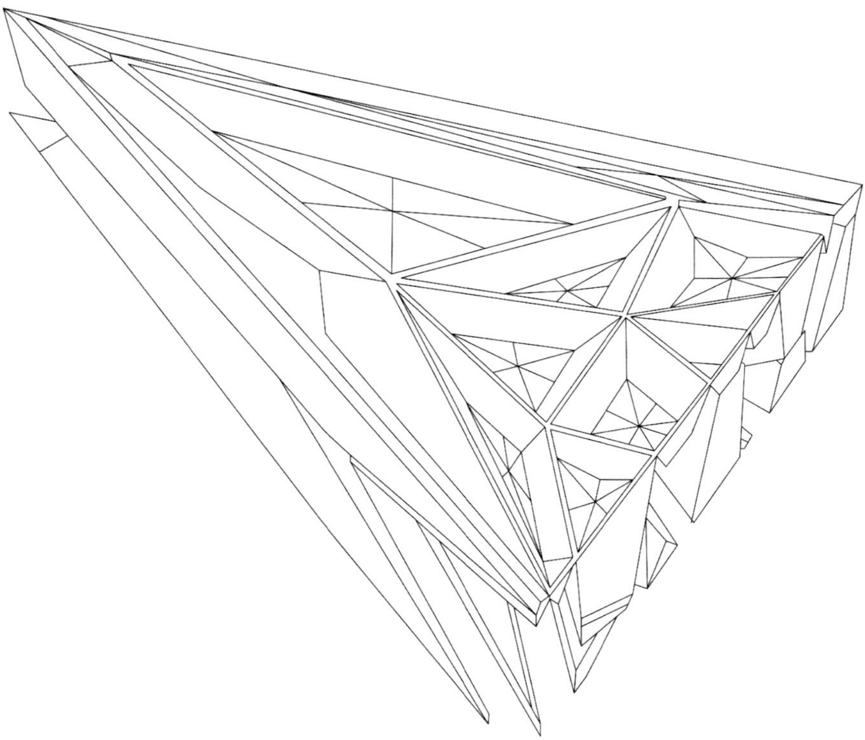

Figure 5.5

This idea is perfectly embodied in various emergent design models that integrate both the organization of design in base of programmed rules and the analysis of the material behavior of the designed object, which according to the complexity paradigm is considered an active factor in the formation of architectural space.

The material computation of architecture

If since the early investigations of performance-based design, the analysis of the behavior of the building has been at the core of different digital design methodologies, emergent design models have taken to another level this design logic in reference to the conception, in natural sciences, of self-organization as the key phenomenon to understand the development of organisms. As explained by Manuel De Landa, this conception of biological development was born when biologists considered that "between the information coded into the genes and the adaptive traits of a plant or animal (i.e., between genotype and phenotype), there are several layers of self-organizing processes, each sustained by endogenously stable states, themselves the product of matter-energy flow."[31]

According to the above idea, which is representative of the penetration of the main subject of second order cybernetics and complexity thinking in natural sciences, in contemporary biology it is considered that genetic material does not exactly constitute "a blueprint for the generation of organic structure and function, an idea implying that genetic materials predefine a form that is imposed on passive flesh. Rather, genes and their products act as constraints on a variety of processes that spontaneously generate order, in a way of *teasing out* a form from active (and morpho-genetically pregnant) flesh."[32] The previous description of biological development has been a main reference for digital architects. In accordance with the description of biological development as a material self-organized system that is constrained by the information contained in the genes, digital designers have imagined new design methodologies grounded on the analysis of the material behavior of the designed object as a generative force in design.

Another aspect of complexity thinking (also representative of the complexity view in biology) has informed the construction of emergent design

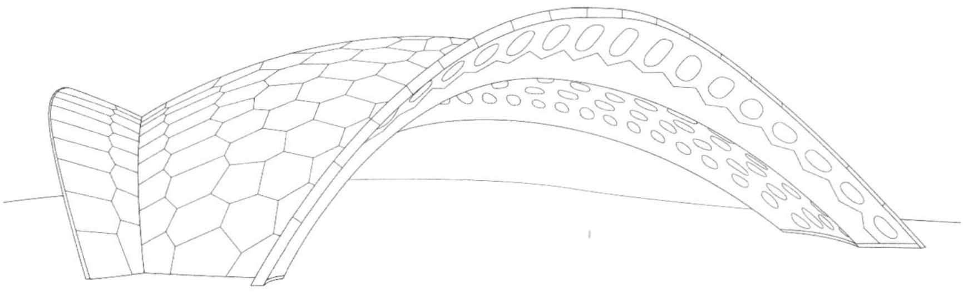

Figure 5.6

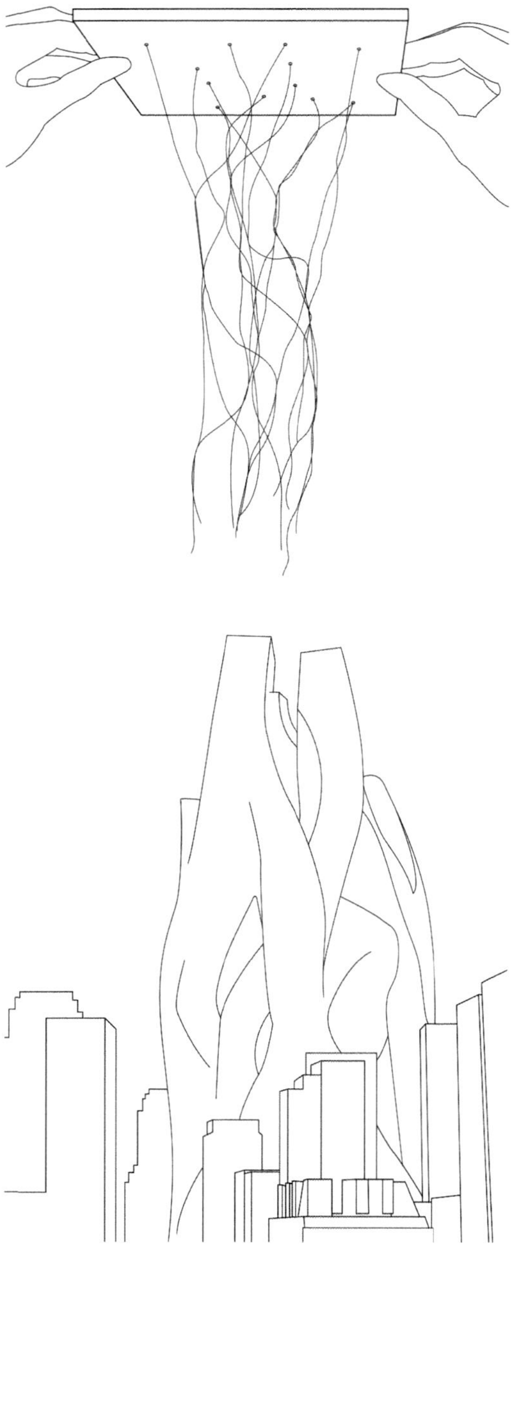

Figure 5.7

models. I refer to the conception of morphogenesis as the capacity of any living system to generate order spontaneously and to create new structures and forms. Complexity thinkers such as Langton, Kaufman, and Wolfram, have considered the abovementioned feature of natural systems as evidence that complex systems display modes of functioning analogue to those of computing. According to Phillip Ball, the use of computer simulations to study natural phenomena is on the basis of the comparison between the mechanisms of life and computing.[33] Ball claims that in contemporary biology several self-organized phenomena are simulated with computational techniques, such as cellular automata, where a series of discreet elements interact according to simple rules. Ball adds that, since in computational simulations of biological phenomena they are described by discrete elements that interact locally with other elements in base of simple rules, scientists have imagined that the natural patterns they observe are the result of a sort of material computation produced by the interaction of the elements of a system.[34] In some recent explorations of emergent design, the morphogenesis of architecture is conceptualized in the same terms. Accordingly, digital architects have fostered design approaches in which the notion of computation is not only related to the programming of the form of the building, but to the comprehension of the physical behavior of the designed object as a sort of material computation from which architectural form emerges (the expansion of this approach in architectural design explains the great interest of some digital architects in the form-finding experiments of architects such as Frei Otto and Antoni Gaudi).

From the above perspective, a series of recent investigations about the morphogenesis of architecture have involved both algorithmic and material computational processes – in which the formation of architecture is considered the result of self-organized processes at different levels, processes that include the programming of form and the simulation and evaluation of its physical behavior. This kind of approach to architectural design implies to think differently of the feedback loops that direct a generative design processes. The consideration of material properties as active generators of form is on the basis of the definition of new uses of computing in design where the material organization of architecture is conceived as the product of feedback loops between the building and the environment that include among the analyzed factors the characteristics and behavior of the material systems that compose the designed object.[35] In this sense, in emergent design models (differently to genetic models) the programming of form is not conceived as the series of instructions that determine the generation of architectural form. Here the programming of architecture defines the restrictions of a variety of procedures that, paraphrasing De Landa, generate order spontaneously, unraveling the architectural form out of active material systems.

An early exploration of the above design approach can be found in the theoretical and experimental work of Lars Spuybroek, one of the key promoters of a theory of generative design that involves the material aspects of the built environment. In agreement with the conception of material behavior as a sort of material computation, the design theory advanced by Spuybroek fosters the consideration of matter as a dynamic entity. Accordingly, in Spuybroek's design research, the material performance of architecture is conceptualized as an active process able to produce order spontaneously. In Spuybroek's words, a design approach informed by the conception of matter as an active system involves the concept of self-organization. From this perspective, matter is an active agent that seeks order, a kind of order that is not transcendentally established but that emerges from the bottom-up.[36] Spuybroek claims that such a conception of design is related to a new (complex) ontology of matter and the potential of computing to explore this ontology. According to the director of NOX, to understand the active properties of matter also implies to consider that any object, be it natural or artificial, is in its origin an organizational singularity that can diverge in multiple real structures. In terms of the design of a building, the former means that the designed object is the product of two phases: a convergence phase and a divergence phase. The convergence phase is "a movement of virtualization, in which information is gathered, selected, graphed or mapped and then organized into a virtual machine." The divergence phase is "a movement of actualization, in which the organizational diagram germinates and becomes formative."[37] In this example, the description of design as a movement of convergence and divergence evokes, once again, an intensive conception of architectural morphogenesis, which is conceived as a process encoded in a program that materializes according to forces inherent to the material system.

The same question can be found in the conception of design advanced by Cecil Balmond in *Element*. Like Spuybroek, Balmond advances a design approach informed by the idea that the formation of natural systems is the result of a feedback process between the information contained in the genes and the forces of the context in which an organism develops. Converted into a praxis of design, the mechanisms of organic development provide Balmond a model for the design of the proper balance between pattern and matter: the algorithm contains the basic design idea and the environment offers the variation possibilities.[38] In other words, what Balmond describes is a design methodology in which the material performance of the building is analyzed and integrated into the feedback loops that define the architectural form in a generative formation process. As in the examples cited above, here the computational production of form involves a movement of virtualization, encapsulated into the program, and a movement of actualization in which matter unfolds its own properties.

The above approach is at the core of the design research of the *Emergence and Design Group*, which, as discussed in the previous chapter, has

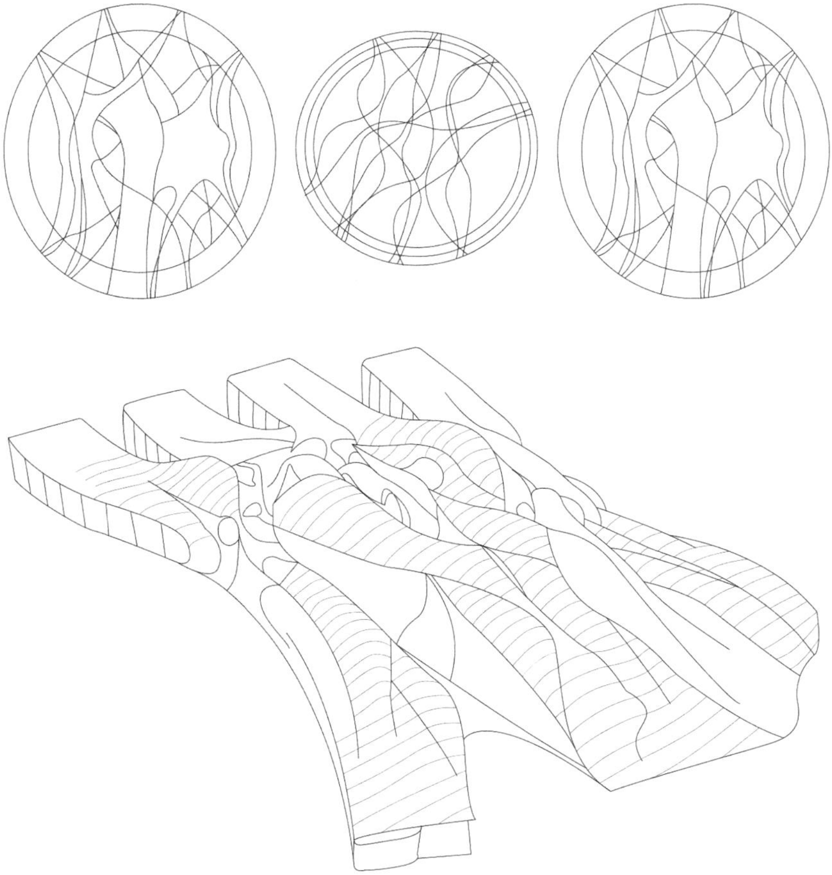

Figure 5.8

explored systemic conceptions of design issues grounded on the idea that the built environment is the product of a spatial-material complex. This idea was further developed by the *Emergence and Design Group* in reference to the complexity paradigm. Under this framework, their investigations also explored an experimental and bio-inspired design methodology grounded on the study of self-organization and emergency in natural systems. According to this framework, Hensel, Menges, and Weinstok studied possible applications in design and digital fabrication of the mechanisms of self-organization (understood as the process that allow systems to increase their order) and emergency (conceptualized as the spontaneous production of different organization levels and interactions among the elements of a system). More precisely, they explored design scenarios informed by the high level of integration and functionality in living beings, and biological strategies such as redundancy and differentiation; these biological concepts describe the mechanisms that guarantee the dynamic interaction of organisms with their environment, their ability to adapt to changing environmental conditions, as well as the processes that permit cells and tissues to evolve toward more specialized functions.[39] In connection with these features of natural systems, the *Emergence and Design Group* established a research program oriented towards the exploration of biological evolution as a significant strategy in design, the production of varied morphologies as a means to generate spaces with different types of organization, as well as the conception of buildings as ecologies; that is, as systems that involve dynamic and varied relations among their parts.[40] These explorations involved the integration into the design process of a series of advances in different fields (including methods to simulate digitally the growth of organisms, computational design and simulation software, digital fabrication machinery, as well as developments in fields such as bio-mimetic engineering, artificial life and material science), which permit to describe the design preferences trough a parametric definition that is informed by a material and environmental context.

In the same line of research, some of the most influential laboratories of digital architecture today investigate design processes, based on the feedback between computational design, advanced simulation and digital fabrication, which explore the possibilities for architectural and structural design of studying the material behavior of natural systems; think, for instance, of the design research promoted by the ITKE and the ICD at the University of Stuttgart. For Achim Menges, head of the ICD, the analysis of the material behavior of the elements of the architectural object (of their mutual relations and of their interaction into a field of external influences) permits a higher integration of designs in multiple levels.[41] In the words of Hensel and Menges, this material approach points towards the construction of architecture as a system able to display higher levels of complex articulation to respond to multiple performance objectives. The former is possible thanks to the integration into the design process of several criteria inherent to the system such as manufacturing and building restrictions, as well as the multiple environmental influences that affect the behavior of the built space.[42]

The material approach to design described above summarizes a new way of thinking about the relationship between form and performance which is inherent to emergent design models. In the early models of performance-based design, the behavior of the building was considered in terms of the feedback among the built space and the surrounding environment. In this sense, a good design is one that solves the appropriate fit among the design requirements and the conditions of a given context. From the perspective of the complexity framework, the good fit is not only achieved through the response of the building to external factors, it comes from within the material organization of the designed object itself, whose behavior is conceived as a sort of physical computational system. As we have seen, emergent design models explore this conception of the morphogenesis of architecture by means of new modes of production of the built space that call to mind the biological description of organic development – which according to the complexity paradigm is as a physical self-organized process. Therefore, emergent models do not consider the performance of architecture as the programmed response of buildings to a series of design variables; in these models, the variables that shape architecture are inner forces that unfold within the environment in which the building takes shape. Paraprhising Clysby, in emergent design processes "we find the distinctive relations between the virtual and the actual as defined by the dual processes of individuation and actualization."[43] The virtual corresponds to "genetic potentiality" as encoded into a program. The development of the architectural form "contains the virtual, genetic potential within it, as *imminent*."[44] Such potential defines the lines along which the actual building forms.

The above is exactly the "intensive" way of thinking that I evoked at the beginning of this chapter. It is a way of thinking about the formation of space in terms of forces flows and processes which, as Leach recalls, is directly connected to the performative line of thought in architecture. As it was discussed in chapter two, the performative view gained momentum with the rise of the computational perspective in architecture, and ever since it has been at the core of the research agenda of digital architects. According to my analysis, the question of the performance of architecture is inseparable from the cybernetic construction of architectural issues, and it has adopted different forms throughout the development of digital architecture – as digital architects have introduced in architectural practice and discourse different concepts and techniques inherited from a variety of fields and theories that make part of the line of thought inaugurated by cybernetics. This is the reason why I claim that the cybernetic framework has directed the development of digital architecture. In this sense, the construction of architectural issues in reference to the complexity paradigm stands out as the latest manifestation of a tradition of cybernetic thinking in the profession that has shaped the imagination of computer-based design for more than 50 years.

According to the above, the complexity view in architecture is particularly representative of a crucial aspect of the explorations of digital architecture that I have tried to show throughout the different chapters of this book. I refer to the fact that to comprehend the techno-scientific trend of digital architecture it is necessary to look at the discourses of information. The informational ascendancy of emergent design models can be clearly observed in the connections that can be established between the use they make of new technologies and the explanations of architectural problems they advance. As we have seen, in emergent models, the development of new design methods based on tools and methods inherited from fields such as bioinformatics, artificial life and material science is justified by a conception of the built environment as an emergent reality, as a sort of developing organism, shaped both by internal and external forces. Here we find the key notions of complexity as scaffolding of the informational ontology and epistemology of architecture which has been systematically explored in computer-based design practices. Beneath the construction of architecture as a complex system appear the usual subjects of the cybernetic view: the conceptualization of the built environment as an ecology, the imagination of buildings as devices that display the characteristics of natural phenomena, the construction of design as a feedback mechanism, and the assessment of the building's behavior as the central aspect of computer-based design processes.

End of the journey

With this look at the complexity view of design issues, I close my journey through the dominant expressions of digital architecture. This journey aimed to present the evolution of the computational perspective in the profession as the product of a feedback process that involves the world of (cybernetic) ideas and the world of (digital) techniques. In this way, I attempted to situate the informational paradigm as the episteme that has defined the intellectual conditions underlying the digital productions of architecture. As we have seen, at the core of the digital turn in architecture are cybernetic narratives that connect the disciplinary problems with a variety of concepts (such as information, code, feedback, homeostasis, system, programming, emergency, self-organization, and complexity) and a series of theories and fields of knowledge (that include operations research, systems theory, genetics, bioinformatics, complexity science, and artificial intelligence) which make part of the line of research inaugurated by the cybernetic paradigm. Through the different chapters, I attempted to traced the origin of these narratives, how they operate in the dominant models that have directed the evolution of digital architecture and to what extent they are connected to the modes of practice of computational design.

At the beginning of this book, I claimed that the mode of analysis of digital architecture described above should provide elements to promote a necessary critical regard of the productions of digital architects. In the next chapter, in guise of conclusion, I analyze the frequent oscillation, in computer-based architectural practices, between the construction of design issues in reference to techno-scientific notions, and the construction of architectural issues as reifications of such resources. This analysis allows me to identify both what I consider some controversial aspects of the digital productions of architecture, as well as possible scenarios for a meaningful cybernetic practice of architecture that is not necessarily trapped, as is frequently the case, into technocratic and reified visions of architectural problems.

Notes

1 See in this respect: Leach, Turnbull, & Williams, *Digital tectonics.*
2 Deleuze, *Différence et répétition.*
3 Clisby, "Intensity in Context," 240.
4 See, in this respect: De Landa, "Space: Extensive and intensive."
5 Warren Weaver was one of the participants of the cybernetic conferences, and he authored the introduction of Claude Shannon's *The Mathematical Theory of communication*, which describes Shannon's work for a non-specialized audience.
6 See in this respect: Weaver, "Science and complexity."
7 See in this respect: Johnson, *Emergence.*
8 See in this respect: Waldrop, *Complexity,* 65.
9 Ibid.
10 Johnson, *Emergence*, 49.
11 Waldrop, *Complexity,* 76.
12 Holland, *Hidden Order: How Adaptation Builds Complexity.*
13 Waldrop, *Complexity,* 12
14 Holland, *Hidden Order: How Adaptation Builds Complexity.*
15 Johnson, *Emergence*, 74.
16 Holland, *Hidden Order: How Adaptation Builds Complexity.*
17 See in this respect: De Landa, *A Thousand Years of Nonlinear History.*
18 Ramage et al., "Editorial: On cybernetics and complexity," 1. See also: Van Dijkum, "From cybernetics to the science of complexity."
19 Alhadeff-Jones, "Three generations of complexity theories."
20 Phelan, "A note on the correspondence between complexity and systems theory," 237.
21 Alhadeff-Jones, "Three generations of complexity theories."
22 Schönwandt et al. *Solving complex problems,* 7.
23 See in this respect: Leach, Turnbull & Williams, *Digital tectonics*, 71.
24 Derix, "Genetically modified spaces," 26.
25 O´Reilly et al., "Emergent Design: Artificial life for architecture." See also: Testa et al., "Emergent Design: a crosscutting research program."
26 Silver, "Automason 1.0."
27 Silver, "Building without drawings," 47.
28 Maciel, "Artificial Inteligence in the conceptualization of Architecture," 62.
29 In the words of Cecil Balmond, the algorithmic design explorations exposed in *Tooling* "compile and reveal a series of embedded orders" that "may hint at cosmic organization; at the micro and realm of compact densities, they intuit biological processes." See, in this respect: Aranda & Lasch, *Pamphlet Architecture 27: Tooling*, 7.
30 Aranda and Lasch, *Pamphlet Architecture 27: Tooling*, 8.
31 De Landa, *A thousand years of nonlinear history*, 112.
32 Ibid.
33 Ball, "Pattern Formation in Nature," 26.
34 Ibid.
35 Menges, "Material computation," 16.
36 Spuybroek, "NOX diagrams," 272.
37 Ibid., 273.
38 Balmond, *Element.*
39 See in this respect: Hensel et al., "Towards self-organisational and multiple-performance capacity in architecture" and Hensel & Menges "Designing Morpho-Ecologies."
40 See in this respect: Hensel & Menges, "Material and digital design synthesis" and Weinstock, "Self-organisation and material constructions."

41 Menges, "Material computation," 20.
42 Hensel & Menges, "Material and digital design synthesis."
43 See note 175.
44 Ibid.

Bibliography

Alhadeff-Jones, Michel. "Three Generations of Complexity Theories: Nuances and Ambiguities." *Educational Philosophy and Theory* 40, no. 1 (2008): 66–82.

Aranda, Benjamin, and Chris Lasch. *Pamphlet Architecture 27: Tooling*. New York: Princeton Architectural Press, 2006.

Ball, Philip. "Pattern Formation in Nature: Physical Constraints and Self-organising Characteristics." *Architectural Design* 82, no. 2 (2012): 22–27.

Balmond, Cecil. *Element*. Munich, Berlin, London, New York: Prestel, 2007.

Clisby, Dale. "Intensity in Context: Thermodynamics and Transcendental Philosophy." *Deleuze Studies* 11, no. 2 (2017): 240–258.

De Landa, Manuel. *A Thousand Years of Nonlinear History*. New York: Swerve Editions, 2000.

De Landa, Manuel. "Material Complexity." In *Digital Tectonics*. Edited by Neil Leach, David Turnbull and Chris Williams, 14–21. Chichester: John Wiley & Sons, 2004.

De Landa, Manuel. "Space: Extensive and Intensive, Actual and Virtual." In *Deleuze and Space*. Edited by Ian Buchanan and Gregg Lambert, 80–88, 2005.

Deleuze, Gilles. *Différence et répétition*. Paris: Presses Universitaires de France, 1968.

Derix, Christian. "Genetically Modified Spaces." In *Space Craft: Developments in Architectural Computing*, 44–53. London: RIBA Publishing, 2008.

Hensel, Michael, and Achim Menges. "Designing Morpho-Ecologies: Versatility and Vicissitude of Heterogeneous Space." *Architectural Design* 78, no. 2 (2008): 102–111.

—. "Material and Digital Design Synthesis." *Architectural Design* 76, no. 2 (2006): 88–95.

Hensel, Michael, Achim Menges, and Michael Weinstock. "Towards Self-organisational and Multiple-Performance Capacity in Architecture." *Architectural Design* 76, no. 2 (2006): 5–11.

Holland, John H. *Adaptation in Natural and Artificial Systems: An Introductory Analysis with Applications to Biology, Control, and Artificial Intelligence*. Cambridge: The MIT Press, 1992.

—. *Hidden Order: How Adaptation Builds Complexity*. New York: Basic Books, 1996.

Johnson, Steven. *Emergence. The Connected Lives of Ants, Brains, Cities and Software*. New York: Scribner, 2001.

Leach, Neil, David, Turnbull, and Chris, Williams. *Digital Tectonics*. Wiley, 2004.

Maciel, Abel. "Artificial Intellignce and the Conceptualisation of Architecture." In *Space Craft: Developments in Architectural Computing*, 60–67. London: RIBA Publishing, 2008.

Menges, Achim. "Material Computation: Higher Integration in Morphogenetic Design." *Architectural Design* 82, no. 2 (2012): 14–21.

O'Reilly, Una M., Ian, Ross, and Peter, Testa. "Emergent Design: Artificial Life for Architecture Design. Artificial Life VII." In *Artificial Life VII*, 454–463. The MIT Press, 2000.

Phelan, Steven E. "A Note on the Correspondence between Complexity and Systems Theory." *Systemic Practice and Action Research* 12, no. 3 (1999): 237–246.
Ramage, Magnus, David Chapman, and Chris Brissell. "Editorial: On Cybernetics and Complexity." *Kybernetes* 42, no. 2 (2013): 1.
Schonwandt, Walter L., Katrin Voermanek, Jurgen Utz, Jens Grunau, and Christoph Hemberger. *Solving Complex Problems. A Handbook*. Berlin: Jovis Verlag GmbH, 2013.
Silver, Mike. "Automason 1.0." *The Journal of Architecture and Computation. http://www.comparch.org.html*, 2005.
—. "Building Without Drawings: Automason Ver 1.0." *Architectural Design* 76, no. 4 (2006): 46–51.
Spuybroek, lars. "NOX Diagrams." In *The Diagrams of Architecture*. Edited by Mark Garcia. Wiley, 2010.
Waldrop, M. Mitchell. *Complexity: the Emerging Science at the Edge of Order and Chaos*. New York: Simon & Schuster, 1992.
Weaver, Warren. "Science and Complexity." *American Scientist* 36 (1948): 536–544.
Weinstock, Michael. "Self-organisation and Material Constructions." *Architectural Design* 76, no. 2 (2006): 34–41.

6 The platonic backhand and forehand of cybernetic architecture

According to my analysis of the cybernetic ascendancy of digital architecture, the research agenda of this field has been deeply influenced by the introduction of informational discourses into the explanations of architecture. As discussed in the previous chapters, this paradigm shift in architectural explanations is on the basis of the development of various design models and methods in which the production of space is considered the result of dynamic processes, a problem solving question, an algorithmic procedure, or a mix of all of the above. As we have seen, these constructions of design issues are closely connected to notions and techniques inherited from a variety of scientific models and theories that are inscribed within the informational paradigm.

Taking into account the above, I have claimed that since the first investigations of computer-based design, digital architecture has been cybernetic. This means that the origins and evolution of digital architecture are not to be considered exclusively as the outcome of the technological developments that have enabled the new architectural expressions that have emerged during the last decades. What this book demonstrates is that, beyond the use of information technology in design practice, those new expressions have usually been the product of rethinking the problems of architecture and design in reference to an informational conception of things. As a matter of fact, from the perspective of New Media studies, the former assertion is a kind of tautology, because the computerization of cultural productions implies what Lev Manovich calls the "transcodification" of cultural categories.[1] For Manovich, this means basically that in computer-mediated cultural productions the replacement of traditional categories does not only stem from the introduction of the pragmatics of the computer as a means of production, but from an informational ontology and epistemology that is inherent to the development of computer technology.[2]

The phenomenon of "transcodification" of the traditional categories of architecture is evident for various architectural theorists and critics who have studied the digital turn in the profession, and who have pointed out the necessity to understand the parallel development of the technical and theoretical aspects that have shaped the development of digital architecture.[3]

DOI: 10.4324/9781003181101-6

Crucially, according to my analysis, such theoretical frameworks have been constructed mainly in reference to ideas and concepts imported from a series of theories and scientific fields directly connected to the cybernetic paradigm. A review of the paradigmatic design models and projects of digital architecture confirms my thesis; namely, that the introduction of computer-based modes of production in architecture has been inseparable from the construction of design issues in reference to the cybernetic view, a framework which expanded to the point of becoming the dominant model of thought in western culture from the mid-twentieth century to the present day. As we have seen along the precedent chapters, the productions of digital architecture embody some of the main transformations in western knowledge promoted by the cybernetic framework. Among such transformations are the widespread conception of things in the world as phenomena whose essence is in the exchange of information, as well as the erasure of the limits between natural and artificial systems fostered by the communicational paradigm. It is by means of this interpretation of the digital productions of architecture that it is possible to understand how architectural objects came to be considered as systems that display the same mechanisms that govern servomechanisms; namely: communication, feedback, programming, self-regulation, etc. Taking the above into account, the main claim of this book is that in the context of the development of a computational perspective in architecture, the informational paradigm has operated both as ontology and pragmatics of the disciplinary problems.

At this point appears the second main element of my argument. Since, according to my analysis, the productions of digital architecture must be considered both as technical systems (grounded on the use information technology) and cultural events (that embody the informational conception of things), they must be thought as the result of a *work of mediation* whose comprehension cannot be limited to the question of the impact of informatics in the profession. Pursuing this idea, the development of the computational perspective in architecture was presented along this dissertation as an example of what N. K. Hayles calls a *seriation*; a term appropriated from archaeological anthropology that describes a mode of analysis of cultural productions that permits to see how the changes in time of a given artifact reveal patterns of overlapping innovation and replication. For Hayles, this method can be applied to study how conceptual shifts "display a seriated pattern reminiscent of material changes in artifacts."[4] According to this mode of analysis, the construction of knowledge can be seen as circular causality system, where the conceptual fields evolve side by side with the transformations of the material culture.[5]

The concept of *seriation* fits perfectly to explain the development of digital architecture, understood as the product of a circular dynamic involving technical and theoretical developments. As we have seen, some of the first explorations of computer-based design appeared concurrently with the informational conception of architectural issues. It was in this way that architects started to conceive of the built environment as a phenomenon that might be explained according to the communicational logic fostered by the cybernetic framework. This idea gave way to the development of new design approaches grounded on data analysis and the elaboration of new explanations of architectural issues informed by information discourses (such as the conception of the built environment as the result of the interaction among several interconnected elements). In turn, these explanations triggered the development of new categories and computer-based design models and so on. According to this circular logic, the evolution of digital architecture can be seen as a feedback process in which the cybernetic imagination of buildings and design issues has fostered the development of computer-based production methods, while the technological mediation of architectural practice has promoted the construction of new cybernetic explanations of disciplinary issues. This logic is at the core of different developments of digital architecture, which are at the crossroads of the exploration of computer technology in design and the explanation of architectural problems in reference to techno-scientific narratives. Among such narratives are the conceptions of architecture as a problem solving discipline and of design as information driven process, as well as the construction of buildings as systems, as genetic mechanisms and as complex phenomena. Within the circular dynamic inherent to the development of digital architecture, the feedback among informational concepts and technologies is the motive force for the permanent development of new theoretical and practical explorations. A good example of the parallel evolution of the technical aspects and the informational imagination of architecture can be observed (in chronological order) in the work of cybernetic architects such as Cedric Price, Christopher Alexander, John Frazer, and Michael Hensel.

The cybernetic constructions of design issues promoted by architects such as Price, Alexander, Frazer, and Hensel are paradigmatic examples which illustrate how the influence of the cybernetic paradigm in architecture can give way to fruitful approaches, which explore new ways of responding to the problems of the production of space that are at the intersection of the use of information technologies in design and the creation of alternative intellectual frameworks for architectural practice. Certainly, among the productions of digital architects it is possible to identify significant explorations that provide new resources to architectural thinking and practice. However, the techno-scientific construction of architectural problems is on the basis of many design explorations and architectural discourses that (more than offering solutions to the problems of architecture) constitute architectural reifications of the references that inspire them. In fact, among the computer-mediated productions of architecture abound the examples of practices that seem to confuse the techno-scientific narratives that inspire them with architecture itself. In consequence, it is not uncommon to observe certain disconnection between the investigations of digital architecture and what I think is the main problem of the profession: the production of significant spaces well adapted to the needs of their users and the conditions of the context in which they are set. As I see it, the productions of digital architecture oscillate between what I consider to be fruitful approaches to architectural issues informed by techno scientific references, and explorations that I consider reified versions of the techno-scientific resources introduced into architectural practice. To define these two trends in digital architecture, I have borrowed another idea from the work of Hayles. Following Hayles, I call the abovementioned oscillation "the platonic backhand and forehand of digital architecture."

Political fiction or science fiction?

According to the two tendencies mentioned before, the explorations of digital architecture can be classified according to two modes of practice in which a "fictional" component plays a central role. I refer to the two categories proposed by the architectural theorist R.E. Somol, who divides architectural practices among those in which the narratives that inspire them can operate as "an idiom of political fiction" and those in which such narratives function as "science fiction rhetoric."[6] According to Somol, the fictional characterization of architectural problems (that is, its formulation in reference to ideological positions, imagination, utopian ideas or, for what matters here, cybernetic notions) is desirable and even a necessity. The fictional construction of design issues is as a way of facing the normative trends that attempt to direct and homogenize contemporary architectural practice. The fictional is a means to imagining alternative scenarios for architectural practice beyond what the *status quo* commands.

However, there are important differences between what Somol calls the *political fiction* approach and the *science fiction* approach. The critic calls *political fiction* the explorations in which the fictional elements are used to describe a mode of practice that is circumscribed into the disciplinary domain of architecture; for instance, when Alexander introduces notions of set theory and systems theory to describe a design approach based on the search of the appropriate fit among the conditions of a given context and the requirements of an architectural problem. In contrast, Somol situates in the category of *science fiction* those architectural practices that foster scientistic visions of design issues. This category describes a trend (quite common in the field of digital architecture) in which architectural problems are substituted by the fictional elements that inspire them; for instance, when architects like Carl Chu and Haresh Lalvani equate the problems of design research with the problems of genetic research. In his article "One Step towards an Ecology of Design," Christopher Hight claims that Somol distrusts the *science fiction* approach because when architects try to mimic scientific models, they make disappear the political dimensions of design.[7]

The opposition between the construction of architectural problems as an idiom of *political fiction* and as *science fiction* rhetoric, that Somol identifies in the work of architects is analogue to a phenomenon detected by Katherine Hayles in the work of scientists. Hayles describes two types of approach to scientific practice that she calls the *platonic backhand* and the *platonic forehand*. The *platonic backhand,* according to Hayles, is the work—characteristic of scientific praxis—that consists in inferring simplified abstractions from the complexity of the world. This was the case, for example, when cyberneticians used the concepts of communication theory as a model to describe diverse phenomena in the world as feedback systems. Hayles considers that problems emerge when this logic is inverted; namely, when scientists employ the abstraction as a substitute of the phenomena that they attempt to explain. A good example of this inverted logic is how some intellectuals have taken the informational explanation of the universe (the world seen as a vast communicational system) for the real phenomenon, leading to reified visions of the informational metaphor (the world conceived as a sort of massive computational program). This kind of move is what Hayles calls the *platonic forehand,* which consists in the reification of the abstractions that scientists use to explain the phenomena they study.[8]

Interestingly, in the work of digital architects it is usual to find similar moves concerning the use of cybernetic narratives in the construction of design issues. As an example of the *platonic backhand* move, the cybernetic imagination of architectural problems has enabled technologically mediated design scenarios that foster a more complex and more whole comprehension of architectural problems. In this way, according to the cybernetic conception of things, the architectural object has been reimagined as a system that is not only constituted by material and spatial aspects, but by complex relations that involve a variety of factors that include the environment and the inhabitants. This idea has reinforced the conception of the built space as an ecology, an approach to the problems of design and construction which is undoubtedly urgent today.

Concurrently, in the best *platonic forehand* style, many cybernetic explorations of architectural problems have promoted the development of new design methods and formal investigations that reflect, above any political consideration, a fascination with the organic, the complex and the intricate character of the scientific phenomena that inspire them. Take, for instance, the vast amount of projects published during the last two decades in a journal such as *Architectural Design.* Among many of the investigations presented in the journal, architecture (or more precisely, the problems of architecture) disappears among a variety of visions regarding the creation of protocellular, evolutionary, and neoplasmatic objects (that look exactly like protocellular, evolutionary, and neoplasmatic objects); in my opinion this kind of exploration keeps a rather imprecise relation with the concrete problem of architecture, that is, the creation meaningful inhabitable spaces.

A common trend among what I consider the *platonic forehand* type explorations of digital architecture, is their penchant towards the definition of modes of practice that privilege the architectural translation of scientific and technological concepts over the solution of concrete design problems. In this kind of practice, it is not uncommon that in the attempt to create a cybernetic architecture (that is, autonomous, self-regulated, self-organized, and emergent buildings), the problem of making meaningful spaces is neglected. In the same way, in the attempt to formulate architectural problems in reference to techno-scientific notions, these architectures of science fiction tend to confuse architectural objects with the scientific objects that they are meant to evoke.

Although it seems judicious to think that in the elaborations of digital architecture scientific inspired design should work in a metaphorical sense, in this field design issues have often been obscured by the techno-scientific narratives underlying the emergence of computer-based design models. Evidently, it is not the same to employ a biological metaphor (genetic coding, for instance) to construct a systemic approach to design issues grounded on the use of programming techniques, as thinking of buildings literally as genetically encoded organisms that grow, evolve and self-replicate. The difference between the two approaches is not a minor matter. While the first approach can help to construct design methods and frameworks that respond to real and concrete architectural needs, the second approach, in my opinion, can only create confusion.

The same type of oscillation can be observed in terms of the technological mediation of design, a phenomenon that is probably the outcome of the reification of the techno-scientific discourses that lie behind many expressions of digital architecture. The implementation of computer-based design processes is usually presented by digital architects as a means to produce architectures capable of displaying the attributes of cybernetic, systemic, self-regulated, and emergent phenomena. Presumably, a building with such attributes should resolve adequately the relation among the various factors involved in the production of the built environment. However, in digital architecture practices it is not unusual that the technological mediation of design is oriented to the exhibition of complex computational, technical and geometric gymnastics that prevail over the solution of the proper relations among the diverse factors that define the qualities of the built environment.

Of course, it can be claimed, in defense of the explorations of the *platonic forehand* type, that they privilege an experimental approach and that, in consequence, they do not seek to offer answers to clearly identified problems but that they are open inquiries that might eventually find (or not find) an application in real and concrete architectural problems. The way I see it, from the perspective of the modes of relation that digital architecture practices establish with the world of science and technology, they can be classified in two groups: those that attempt to define an architectural agenda in reference to techno-scientific notions and those that reduce architectural expressions to reifications of the techno-scientific resources they evoke. While some investigations of digital architecture explore the technological mediation of design as a means to foster a truly cybernetic praxis of architecture, in other cases the use of technological and scientific tools becomes an end in itself. In these cases, the definition of a technological agenda for architecture has tended to become autonomous from the network of social, cultural, politic, economic and material factors that take part in the definition of any spatial reality. The problem of such disconnection is that it can easily lead to technocratic visions of architectural issues that recreate the simplifications of the discourses of technological determinism: the belief in a possible future in which the urging global problems of the urbanized world will be solved by intelligent machines, self-building architectures, etc. It is somewhat disturbing to realize that this kind of discourse underlays the research subjects of many students of computational design programs, as well as the research projects of many of their instructors.

I suggested before that probably the above mentioned disconnection (along with the technocratic derives of digital architecture) is the result of the reification of architectural issues. My take is that when the narratives that influence the productions of architecture (the cybernetic imagination of design) replace the concrete problems of design (the production of meaningful spaces), it comes as no surprise that the investigations of digital architecture keep an imprecise relationship with the problem of making good architecture (be it cybernetic or not). However, this disconnection is not inevitable, and certainly it should not be considered as the necessary outcome of a technologically mediated practice of architecture – although not everybody agrees on this point.[9] As a matter of fact, the informational ontology and epistemology of architecture can offer valuable tools (both theoretical and technical) for a practice of the profession that is not necessarily locked into technocratic and reified conceptions of architectural issues. Yet, to avoid such dead ends, it is fundamental that digital architects take up a critical attitude towards the practice – and history – of computer-mediated architecture.

A critical tool

Nearly 30 years ago, two of the key promoters of the use of new technologies in design warned us about the importance of adopting a critical attitude regarding the development of the computational perspective in architecture. In *Digital Design Media,* an influential book that marked a whole generation of digital designers, William Mitchell and Malcom McCullough claimed that it is only possible to assume a critical position if one understands the conditions that have structured the intellectual work of digital architects.[10] In a way, my research about the role of the cybernetic model in digital architecture is a response to the advice of Mitchell and McCullough. By situating cybernetic thinking as the key factor that has structured the evolution of digital architecture, the survey presented in this book allows the reader to assess the significance of the informational paradigm for the development of the dominant visions of digital architecture until the present day. More importantly, the comprehension of this influence should permit the reader to identify both the fertile and controversial aspects of the construction of architectural problems in reference to the ideas and techniques that have shaped digital culture.

As I write these final words, I see the call for a critical approach, on which Mitchell and McCullough insisted, as a warning against the reification of the informational approach in architecture, a drift that, as we have seen, can lead to the autonomization of the technical explorations of digital architects from the concrete matters of architecture. This warning is as relevant today as it was back in the early 1990s, when Mitchell and McCullough wrote *Digital Design Media*. The reason is that in a global society that trusts deeply in technological advance as the solution to the pressing problems that we face today (global warming, global pandemic, global precariousness), it is easy for architects to fall under the spell of the promises of technological development; namely, the arrival of technologically mediated architectures that will eventually achieve biology and that, as living organisms or, more precisely, like von Neumann's self-replicating automata, will attain the self-organizing capacities they need to design and construct themselves. These visions of the computerization of architecture constitute the axes that have directed the explorations of many digital architects, whose work revisits the utopian spirit of the architectural avant-garde of the early twentieth century. Such visions are the translation into architectural idioms of the ideals of the pioneers of computer science and cybernetics, who shared the conviction that information technology held the key for the creation of intelligent machines, the production of artificial systems able to emulate the reproductive and adaptive capacities of living systems, and ultimately, to make a surrogate of the human being, a perfect slave capable of replacing humans in a series of annoying tasks.

Despite the preeminence of these ideas in the work of many digital architects, there are other possible readings of the cybernetic paradigm that can provide insights for a meaningful architectural practice that is not trapped into technocratic visions of the disciplinary problems. Certainly, the fathers of cybernetics shared with computer scientists a series of ideas that lie behind the dreams of automation and artificial intelligence that are at the core of the developments of information technology. The cybernetitians interest in studying problems of control, regulation, programming and feedback, and their belief that the functioning of information processing machines was equivalent to that of living systems make part of this research agenda. As a matter of fact, early cybernetitians such as William Ross Ashby and William Grey Walter invented artifacts, like the homeostat and the electric tortoise, that at their time were ground breaking advances in the field of information technology. However, behind these shared research interests, there is a radical difference between the work of computer scientists and cybernetitians. While computer scientists were mainly interested in the production of computing machines, the scope of the cybernetitians agenda was larger. As discussed in the introduction to this book, the ultimate aim of cybernetitians was to construct a framework to study and explain several phenomena in the world as information exchange processes. Their objects of study were those systems (either natural or artificial) capable of self-regulating their behavior due to their ability to process information they receive from their environment, and whose action, inversely, has an impact on their surroundings. Accordingly, cybernetic theory fostered a framework to analyze diverse phenomena as communicational forms of organization, as feedback systems whose actions produce changes on their environment, that subsequently trigger changes on them.

When it comes to think of the problems of the production of space, I find this framework far more powerful than the promises of intelligence and automation that the computerization of architecture offers. What the cybernetic framework offers is a means to analyze design problems from a holistic perspective, independently from the technical means involved in such analysis. In this regard, it is interesting to remind that Christopher Alexander, one of the pioneers of cybernetic architecture, has claimed that the most relevant aspect of his informational conception of design (as presented in his well-known essay *Notes on the Synthesis of Form*) is not connected to the technical aspects of the method he describes. A few years after the publication of the book, Alexander wrote that he had come to the conclusion that the crucial finding of *Notes on the Synthesis of Form* is that architectural objects can be described as the set of relationships that define a system of interconnected forces. In the preface to the 1973 edition of the book, Alexander explains this idea as follows: "The idea that it is possible to create such abstract relationships one at a time, and to create designs which are whole by fusing these relationships – this amazingly simple idea is, for me, the most important discovery of the book."[11]

The further investigations developed by Alexander reinforce the idea that the main contribution of cybernetic thinking to architecture is a framework for thinking the built environment from a holistic perspective. This idea is central to the vast research presented in *A Pattern Language,* where the authors state that "when you build a thing you cannot merely build that thing in isolation, but must also repair the world around it, and within it, so that the larger world at that one place becomes more coherent, and more whole; and the thing which you make takes its place in the web of nature, as you make it."[12]

At a time when the computerization of design appears as a sort of new avant-garde of architecture,[13] the voices of Alexander and his colleagues should be listened to carefully. In my opinion, their systemic conception of space is the best instance of the cybernetic construction of architecture as *political fiction*. It is a *platonic backhand* move that addresses cybernetic notions to promote a mode of practice of design that responds specifically to the problem of making good inhabitable spaces. It is also a good example of how the introduction into architectural knowledge of ideas and concepts imported from external scientific fields (such as systems analysis and systems theory) does not necessarily lead to the construction of architectural issues as a *science fiction* rhetoric. Alexander's attitude towards the construction of a fictional framework for architecture inspired by cybernetic concepts is the exact opposite of the reified and technocratic constructions of architectural problems – as fostered by explorations of the *platonic forehand* type, where the cybernetic metaphors devised to explain architectural issues take the place of architecture itself.

A look at the evolution of digital architecture reveals that the informational construction of architecture can be a valuable framework to rethink design problems. This framework can provide interesting tools to conceive architectural expressions able to address the complex set of conditions and factors implicated in the production of space. From the above it follows that the *science fiction* drifts of digital architecture are not the necessary outcome of thinking new scenarios for architectural practice informed by information discourses and technologies. These drifts are the consequence of pursuing a mode of practice in which the techno-scientific resources introduced into architectural knowledge become autonomous from the concrete problems that architects must solve. To avoid such disconnection, my advice to the designers interested in the technological mediation of architecture is to practice their backhand stroke; in this sense, the study the intellectual conditions that have shaped the evolution of digital architecture is a critical tool.

In a way, this book tells a history of how the ideals of automation, control, self-regulation, and artificial intelligence inherent to the development of information technology and information discourses migrated to architecture, shaping new visions and modes of practice of the profession. This history should help the reader to grasp where do these ideals come from, how they materialize in the discourses, methods and objects produced by digital architects and, more importantly, to judge if they offer appropriate answers to the question of what should be the aim of a truly cybernetic architecture: building more coherent, and more whole places.

Notes

1 Manovich, *The Language of New Media*.
2 Crucially, the scholars that have studied the history of computer science have produced enough evidence that the development of the computer is a cultural project that involves both technological and ideological aspects, and that such ideological aspects are inseparable from the emergence of the informational paradigm.
3 Among the architectural scholars who have pointed out the necessity to establish the connections between the parallel development of the technical and theoretical aspects of digital architecture are Antoine Picon, Christopher Hight, Sean Keller, Altino Joao Rocha, Daniel Cardoso Llach, Reinhold Martin, and Molly Wright Steenson, among others.

4 See in this respect, Hayles, *How We Became Posthuman*, 14.
5 Hayles, for instance, uses this method to explain the parallel evolution between the key cybernetic ideas and the appearance of paradigmatic cybernetic artifacts, such as William Ross Ashby's Homeostat or William Grey Walter's Tortoise.
6 See in this respect: Somol, "Cartoon Plan". Lecture given at Ohio State University (21 October 2009); see also: Somol, "Lessity, More – ism." Lecture given at Rice School of Architecture (12 April 2010).
7 Hight, "One Step towards an Ecology of Design."
8 Hayles, *How We Became Posthuman,* 12–13.
9 For instance, the influential architectural critic like Kenneth Frampton has shown his skepticism in this sense. Indeed, he has claimed that the technological mediation of architecture is a dead end. See in this respect: Frampton, "Arquitectura y Vanguardia." See also my response to Frampton's arguments in: Cifuentes Quin, "Arquitectura y computación."
10 Mitchell & McCullough, *Digital Design Media.*
11 Alexander, *Notes on the Synthesis of Form.*
12 Alexander et al., *A Pattern Language,* xiii.
13 Notice that among the architects awarded the Pritzker Prize in architecture during the last two decades, many of them have been important promoters, or precursors, of digital design (Frei Otto, Zaha Hadid, Norman Foster, Thom Mayne, Frank Ghery), while others have enthusiastically introduced computational design concepts and techiniques in some of their most iconic projects (Shigeru Ban, Rem Koolhas, Toyo Ito, Jean Nouvel, Herzog, & de Meuron).

Bibliography

Alexander, Christopher. *Notes on the Synthesis of Form.* Cambridge, MA: Harvard University Press, 1973.

Alexander, Christopher, Sara Ishikawa, and Murray Silverstein. *A Pattern Language. Towns, Buildings, Construction.* Oxford: Oxford University Press, 1977.

Cifuentes Quin, Camilo. "Arquitectura y computación ¿determinismo o mediación?: del paradigma informacional hacia una tectónica digital." *Dearq* no. 10 (2012): 22–35.

Frampton, Kenneth. "Arquitectura y Vanguardia." *Lecture given at Caixa Forum Barcelona.* 2011.

Hayles, N. Katherine. *How We Became Posthuman: Virtual Bodies in Cybernetics, Literature and Informatics.* Chicago: The University of Chicago Press, 1999.

Hight, Christopher. "One Step towards an Ecology of Design." In *Design Innovation for the Built Environment. Research by Design and the Renovation of Practice.* Edited by Michael Hensel. London: Routledge, 2012.

Manovich, Lev. *The Language of New Media.* Cambridge, Mass: The MIT Press, 2001.

Mitchell, William, and Malcom, McCullough. *Digital Design Media.* New York: Van Nostrand Reinhold, 1995.

Somol, Robert. "Cartoon Plan." *Lecture given at Ohio State University.* 2009.

—. "Less -Ity, More -Ism." *Lecture given at Rice School of Architecture.* 2010.

Table of figures

Index

For Product Safety Concerns and Information please contact our EU representative GPSR@taylorandfrancis.com Taylor & Francis Verlag GmbH, Kaufingerstraße 24, 80331 München, Germany

Batch number: 10722122

Printed by Printforce, the Netherlands